Consciousness Literature & the Arts 34

General Editor:
Daniel Meyer-Dinkgräfe

Editorial Board:
Anna Bonshek, Per Brask, John Danvers,
William S. Haney II, Amy Ione,
Michael Mangan, Arthur Versluis,
Christopher Webster, Ralph Yarrow
Jade Rosina McCutcheon

Reading Coetzee

Elizabeth MacFarlane

Rodopi

Amsterdam - New York, NY 2013

Cover illustration: *Before the Law* (2013) by Yoshua Wakeham. Licensed under the Creative Commons Attribution-ShareAlike 3.0 Unported License.

Cover design by Aart Jan Bergshoeff.

The paper on which this book is printed meets the requirements of "ISO 9706:1994, Information and documentation - Paper for documents - Requirements for permanence".

ISBN: 978-90-420-3701-4
ISSN: 1573-2193
E-Book ISBN: 978-94-012-0958-8
E-book ISSN: 1879-6044
© Editions Rodopi B.V., Amsterdam - New York, NY 2013
Printed in the Netherlands

This book is dedicated to my mentor Kevin Brophy.

Acknowledgements

I would like to acknowledge the School of Culture and Communication and the Faculty of Arts at the University of Melbourne for providing me with the time and resources to complete this work.

I would like to thank my parents, Jeff and Carol, for their unwavering and generous support. And my son Henry who is too young to read, but old enough to know that books create the world.

Parts of this book have been previously published in different forms in:
TEXT: Journal of Writing and Writing Courses (October 2011); *New Scholar: An International Journal of the Humanities, Creative Arts and Social Sciences* (September 2011); *New Antigone* (2006) and *Traffic: An interdisciplinary postgraduate journal* (2006).

Contents

Introduction

This book presents an analysis of J. M. Coetzee's body of work with a focus on his linked pair of 'post-Nobel' novels *Elizabeth Costello* and *Slow Man*. Just as Coetzee's recent books often present essays and narrative alongside one another, this book engages with its ideas through both critical and creative writing. *Reading Coetzee* interleaves critical essays on Coetzee's works with a thread of autobiographical narrative detailing a more personal response to my reading and writing. It also includes a collection of short fiction which was written in direct response to some of the themes and threads found in analysing Coetzee's work. The presentation of elements of the creative with the critical, and the critical within the creative, aims to challenge the traditional boundaries between the two methods of engagement. The overriding viewpoint behind this kind of methodology speaks to the idea of embodiment: that an idea or philosophy does not 'float free', but is tied to the idiosyncrasies, divergences, and subjective 'travel' of its speaker or writer. The critical-creative nexus is thus both an exploration in the limits of form or genre, and an examination of the divided consciousness of the writer who is at once a particular person and a conduit; both continuing in time and existing (through their work) in time's rupture.

When I was first deciding on a topic for my doctoral thesis in 2003, I read J. M. Coetzee's novel *Elizabeth Costello*, and saw immediately that what he was doing to both the novel form and the essay form was something that could sustain a three-year project. It's a book with a writer-thinker protagonist Costello who travels around presenting lectures; we read both these lectures and the surrounding story of her travels, family and memories. Thus the reader is presented with something which we very rarely see in novels or in the academy: both the conference paper, or academic journal article, *and* the very specific human circumstances surrounding its writing and delivery.

Feminist scholars like Jane Tompkins, Rachel Blau DuPlessis, Anne Carson, the University of Canberra's Jen Webb and many others have taken up this position and produced texts which challenge the traditional dichotomy between academic and creative writing.

Derrida once wrote: "We must invent [a name] for those "critical" inventions which belong to literature while deforming its limits" (Derrida 1992b: 52), and although the name itself has proven decidedly difficult to pin down (some terms have been: autocritography, fictocriticism, theory-fiction, critifiction, paracriticism and research fiction), the notion of deforming the limits of form and genre, splicing critical and creative writing together, producing texts in which the two are actually inextricable, allowing autobiography and the personal voice to inform literary theory, these practices have flourished, if somewhat quietly, and are indeed cornerstones of creative writing practice, research and pedagogy within the academy. I share Jen Webb's view when she writes: "If we continue to separate poetry and philosophy, then we lose the potential offered by each" (2009), and Giorgio Agamben's "every authentic poetic project is directed toward knowledge, just as every authentic act of philosophy is always directed toward joy" (1993: xvii).

I have also adopted ideas like those in Jane Tompkins' seminal essay 'Me and my shadow' which argue that traditional academic writing, in its tone and level, involves what she calls a pretence: the pretence that "epistemology, or whatever you're writing about, has nothing to do with your life, that it's more exalted, more important, because it (supposedly) *transcends* the merely personal" (2131). She goes on to write,

> The claim of this language I've been using (and am using right now) lies in its implicit deification of the speaker. Let's call it the 'authority effect'. I cannot describe the pretense except to talk about what it ignores: the human frailty of the speaker, his body, his emotions, his history; the moment of intercourse with the reader – acknowledgement of the other person's presence, feelings, needs. This 'authoritative' language speaks as though the other person weren't there. (Tompkins: 2136).

An epigraph to one of this book's chapters from Coetzee's novel *Diary of a Bad Year* reflects a similar attitude: "There is a tone – I don't know the best word to describe it – a tone that really turns people off. A know-it-all tone. Everything is cut and dried: *I am the one with all the answers, here is how it is, don't argue, it won't get you anywhere"* (2007a: 57. Original ital.).

Thus in my own critical work, I seek to present writing that I, after Coetzee, call 'embodied'. In an authorial interjection in Lesson One of *Elizabeth Costello* we read: "The notion of *embodying* turns out to be pivotal. In such debates ideas do not and indeed cannot float free: they are tied to the speakers by whom they are enounced" (2003a: 9). This notion that ideas are always necessarily tied to people, to bodies, is equally applicable to creative writing as it is to critical writing. My position is that all writing is built of an exchange or dialogue, often between two parts of the self: the public and private self, for example, or the self as writer and the self as reader; the self that explains or tells things, and the self that simply lives or enacts them. Many texts attempt to sever one from the other, as with academic writing which cuts away the personal 'I', the anxiety of the rejoinder, the concrete everyday details that have triggered the ideas in the first place. And as with the creative writing that follows the 'laws' of 'show don't tell' and Richard Hugo's "think small... if you can't think small, try philosophy or social criticism" (1979: 7) so that characters and events are presented as a series of actions and objects without pause for self-reflection, or philosophy. Hybrid writing, as an alternative, acknowledges the exchange, and indeed celebrates it. In a university discipline where students are taught to both think critically about creative texts, and to produce their own creative texts, I believe that allowing for ways in which the two modes might intersect is an important part of the academic's work.

There are, of course, dangers that go along with this position. Jen Webb puts it eloquently:

> We place metaphor in general and symbolic (creative) writing at that end of the (academic) writing continuum which has low modal value – or little apparent transparency to 'reality'. In philosophical or academic terms, creative writing has the lowest modality, and hence the lowest truth claim, because it has the least apparent transparency. This means that those of us who are also academics, and yearn to write in that liminal space between philosophy and poetry, always risk the 'contamination' of the creative – and its low modality – when read by academics, and risk the 'contamination' of the critical – and its insistent reason – when read by creative writers. (Webb: 2009)

As with any hybrid-born, the danger is that the structures of success are usually decided upon by those registered as 'pure' species.

Like Webb, I have found that pursuing the place of metaphor in writing has proven to be a useful hinge upon which to open new spaces of meaning when speaking about the critical-creative nexus. Particularly useful to me in my analysis of the book *Elizabeth Costello* was the fact that Peter Singer, a very famous modern philosopher, wrote and delivered a response to one of its chapters, the Lives of Animals. Singer, in a sort of up-ending of Coetzee's incursions into philosophical thought, wrote the lecture as a piece of fiction, mostly consisting of a third-person dialogue between himself and his daughter Naomi. During the conversation, and like many philosophers, Singer uses analogies to explain his points more clearly. The piece was valuable to me because even though it might have been described as hybrid in terms of its form, it was very clearly not built out of the exchange or dialogue within the self I referred to earlier. Its sole purpose was to refute Coetzee's book on philosophical grounds, and it used its fictional scaffolding as a further ploy to do this. Singer does not enter or embody his characters.

Reading Coetzee's presentation of critical and creative writing alongside one another speaks to a number of broad concerns of contemporary consciousness studies, including the relationship between ideas and emotions, the necessary shift between embodiment and exclusion (the impression of a 'unified' or 'split' self), and the writer's distinct willingness to accept, even establish, anxiety and contradictions as part of her work.

Elizabeth Costello, Slow Man and *Diary of a Bad Year* explicitly address themes which abide more surreptitiously throughout J. M. Coetzee's oeuvre: the divisions and paradoxes which occur the moment pen gains page, the value of literature, and the ethics of embodiment. In revealing the dialogue between writer-self and reader-self, and between author and character, they invite a rereading of Coetzee's previous literature. This book explores Coetzee's preoccupation with the act of writing using his recent books as a lens through which to view his eight previous novels as well as his memoirs and essays.

The book is organised into four main chapters – 'This Book is Irregular', 'Metaphor as Contagion,' 'The Author Divided,' and 'The

Ethics of Embodiment' – followed by a collection of short fiction, a concluding chapter and a Postscript.

'This Book is Irregular' uses Coetzee's 1984 essay 'A Note on Writing' and its introduction of the concept of 'the middle voice' as a framework for an extensive discussion of the critical-creative nexus, and the implications of writing a book of literary criticism in this mode. This section also provides an outline of the shifts in the focus of 'Coetzee criticism' over the last twenty years, and an idea of the broader critical landscapes which have informed *Reading Coetzee*'s conceptual framework, including: Blanchot's ideas on ambiguity; Calinescu's concept of re-reading; Said's term 'late style' to refer to works produced towards the end of an artist's career or life; and the recurring image of the blank page in Coetzee's oeuvre.

'Metaphor as Contagion' engages with the Postscript of *Elizabeth Costello* with the intention of introducing the concept that Coetzee's late works (since 2003) act as 'postscripts' to his previous body of writing. It proposes that every act of writing, as particularly demonstrated in the suspended poetics of metaphor and analogy, is an act of sacrifice, as evinced by Lady Chandos in Coetzee's Postscript: *"Always it is not what I say, but something else!"* Citing Blanchot, Lacan, Jakobson and Pierre Macherey alongside poet Charles Simic, novelist Italo Calvino, and Coetzee himself, this chapter observes the deficiency of language, the writer's attempt nonetheless, and the inevitable resultant ruptures in text and self.

'The Author Divided' argues that one reason for the unbearable nature of the moment of writing is that it prompts a divide within the author. The divisions explored in this chapter include: the author as both continuing in time and existing in time's rupture; the author as both particular person and common passageway, the author as both enacting a performance of literature and catching glimpses of the Law of literature, and following this, the author as both human and divine. The complex divisive relationship between author and character is also explored, particularly in relation to *Slow Man*, *Foe* and *Age of Iron*. Edward Said's concept of 'late style' is utilised in this chapter to explore the often negative critical reaction to Coetzee's Costello books, which are seen as anachronistic to the post-postmodern novel and anathema to his 'Booker books' *Life and Times of Michael K* and *Disgrace*. Coetzee writes in *Diary of a Bad Year*, "Language cannot get purchase, cannot get going, until it has split up the unity of experience" (2007a: 49). Citing Kafka, Derrida, Schelling and Zižek, this chapter traces the divisions within the consciousness of every text as erupting from the splitting of white page into marked page.

'The Ethics of Embodiment' argues that questions of ethics, and the responsibility of the writer, are necessarily entangled with questions of metaphor and embodiment. Alongside the work of philosophers such as Peter Singer, Thomas Nagel and Mary Midgley, it analyses Coetzee's most controversial novels, *Disgrace, Waiting for the Barbarians* and *The Master of Petersburg*. This chapter also delves into questions of the self-consciousness of animals, and Coetzee's widely-cited argument comparing animal slaughter to the genocide of the Holocaust. It concludes that the immersion and emergence from embodiment is a cycle which demonstrates that both fiction and life are simultaneously real and imagined.

As will be explained in greater detail in the following chapter, the short stories and autobiographical 'interruptions' included in this book were written alongside, often in direct response to the themes and ideas discussed in the literary criticism.

This Book is Irregular:
On the critical-creative nexus

There is a tone – I don't know the best word to describe it – a
tone that really turns people off. A know-it-all tone. Every-
thing is cut and dried: I am the one with all the answers, here
is how it is, don't argue, it won't get you anywhere.
I know that isn't how you are in real life, but that is how you
come across, and it is not what you want.
If you positively have to write about the world and how you
see it, I wish you could find a better way.
J. M. Coetzee in *Diary of a Bad Year*

The premise of my argument over the course of this discussion of J.
M. Coetzee's novels and essays is that although the characters, stories
and arguments presented therein could be considered on many levels,
crossing many discourses, there is a persistent underlying question
which in his Elizabeth Costello novels (*Elizabeth Costello* and *Slow
Man*) is brought into the clear to be examined. It is the question of the
value of literature – a question which addresses the excruciating moment between not writing and writing. I will address these issues by
asking of the novels: What makes this moment problematic? How
does the identity, responsibility and suffering of the writer factor in to
Coetzee's question about the value or *good* of literature? And how
does this writerly 'moment' transfer onto the written page and then to
the reader?

What Coetzee is presenting us with in *Elizabeth Costello* is a
series of arguments which, when taken together, cannot be responded
to, as many reviewers have discovered, as controversial polemics on
animal rights or the problem of evil. Peter Singer realized this when
he responded to Coetzee's Princeton lectures on the Lives of Animals
– lectures which now make up two chapters of the novel. He discov-

ered that the terms for any response were dictated by Coetzee's writing. In the end, Singer responded in the only way possible, using a fictional dialogue between himself and his daughter finishing with the exchange: "'Pretty tricky. Not an easy thing to reply to. But why don't you try the same trick in response?' '*Me*? When have I ever written fiction?'" (Singer 1999: 91). Not only has Singer never written fiction, he has never written self-reflexive tricky fiction, a marvel brought about by Coetzee's refusal to delineate fiction from theory. Singer criticises Coetzee's method as "a marvellous device," going on to point out the safety of ambiguity: "Costello can blithely criticize the use of reason, or the need to have any clear principles or proscriptions, without Coetzee really committing himself to these claims" (91). I will argue, however, that Coetzee's cunning 'device' of presenting a fictional narrative as a frame surrounding theoretical contentions is not only interesting and clever, but is an inevitable consequence of the nature of Costello's lectures and debates and, behind them, Coetzee's interrogation of the value of literature. As Singer himself admits as co-editor of the compilation *The Moral of the Story: An Anthology of Ethics through Literature* (Singer 2005: x-xi), philosophical illustrations as "thought-experiments" and literature as "a more nuanced view of character and circumstance" rarely share a page or even a language. Intertwining fiction and argument is itself a line of reasoning, an argument; or perhaps an anti-argument.

The middle voice
In his short essay 'A Note on Writing' Coetzee discusses what he calls 'the middle voice' – the voice that exists between the active and the passive:

> The phantom presence of a middle voice…can be felt in some senses of modern verbs if one is alert to the possibility of the threefold opposition active-middle-passive. 'To write' is one of these verbs. To write (active) is to carry out the action without reference to the self…To write (middle) is to carry out the action (or better, to do-writing) with reference to the self. (Coetzee 1984b: 11)

In relation to the recurring discussion in *Elizabeth Costello* between writing/literature and reason/philosophy the notion of the middle voice can be seen as the way in which the writing-act is set apart as a self-generating space. Coetzee goes on to cite Barthes: "The field of writing...has today become nothing but writing itself, not as art for art's sake but as the only space there is for the one who writes" (1992: 95). When using a term like 'anti-argument' in relation to *Elizabeth Costello*, there are many possible ways of misconstruing it. It is not used, for instance, to refer to the way in which each of Costello's lectures is undercut by various individuals, rendering her conclusions and passion ambiguous. It is not used either to refer to creative writing in contrast to criticism in the manner of Joel Fineman's essay:

> Because the things of poetry are words, poetry can, in a way that criticism cannot, conclude itself when it cannot continue...it can lapse into significant literary silence, thereby prolonging its desire ad infinitum...But criticism, whose things are not words but the meanings of words, meanings forever foreclosed by words, will find in silence only the impetus for further speech...Whereas a poem can be closed poetically even by a gesture of self-abandon, criticism, discovering the futility of its project, can only go on and on, frustratingly repeating its own frustration. (Fineman 1981: 50)

Although this distinction is an important one when analysing the interaction of form and content, the term 'anti-argument' goes even further into Coetzee's definition of the middle voice *as having reference to the self*. The way in which commentators treat 'Costello' and 'Coetzee' as interchangeable authors raises further questions regarding the purity of author-identity and the blurring of self with writing. In the two books, *Elizabeth Costello* and *Slow Man*, the image of the writer is doubled, from Costello to Coetzee. And, to take Blanchot's striking impression in a literal sense, a quadrupled image, as each writer "is proof that within one individual there exist side by side both a man full of dread and one who is cool and calculating, both a madman and a reasonable being, a mute who has lost all words firmly wedded to an orator, master of discourse" (1999: 346). The term anti-argument refers to the writer as much as to the writing-act. Peter Singer seems to demonstrate this double image when, on the one hand, his philosophy regarding the value of human life displays an icy logic, while on the other, he cannot explain with the same logic his firm knowledge that he would give a Down syndrome child born to him up for adoption immediately. Putting aside the ethical heart of this situation, it is possible to see the conflict between Singer's extraneous image and his internal 'anti-argument' (Singer 2004).

In my own response to the texts, this double-image of the writer (my name being very useful here) has become this book's middle voice through third-person autobiographical pieces which intersect with the critical writing. In a reversal of Coetzee's lecture-within-fiction, these 'fictions-within-criticism' – which eventually culminate in writing-acts, stories – explore, in a practical but not symmetrical way, the concepts and abstractions raised in the surrounding analysis. When 'Elizabeth', in a forthcoming section, seems to find herself in an uncanny nexus of coincidental numbers and events, her idea of this book *Elizabeth Costello* – which is so entangled in the story of its purchase, the images on its cover, the images of her dream – becomes, like a revelation, something beyond her grasp and beyond the grasp of language. She is disappointed with her attempt at fiction – "it thudded from her like a dropped sack" – because at this point in her own development, and the development of the book on Coetzee she is writing, it is too much like a compromise. In a deliberate reference to the blurred image of the writer/character in *Elizabeth Costello*, this book's voice interchanges between narration and lecture, between acting and observing.

All of this manhandling of the writer and the writing voice, from both Coetzee's and this book's perspective, is significant in terms of the central question of the excruciating moment of writing and the value of literature. Just as the middle voice exists as the verb 'to do writing', between activity and passivity, the value of literature is neither wholly beyond the author nor completely contained in the author. As I will elaborate in 'The Author Divided,' Coetzee's developing image of the writer throughout all his previous novels, involves certain doublings and divisions. In each manifestation the author is divided between a being continuing in time and a being existing in time's rupture; between enacting a performance of literature, and catching glimpses of the Law of literature; between being a particular person with body and name, and being a passageway for other voices; between being 'god-like' and 'thing-like'; between being an author and a character. It is in *Elizabeth Costello* and *Slow Man*, acting as jarring 'Postscripts' to Coetzee's formal body of work, that these various divisions are more clearly defined.

Blanchot refers to a similar between-ness in a passage from 'Literature and the Right to Death':

> Let us suppose that literature begins at the moment when litera-
> ture becomes a question...As soon as the page has been written,
> the question which kept interrogating the writer while he was
> writing – though he may not have been aware of it – is now pre-
> sent on the page; and now the same question lies silent within the
> work, waiting for a reader to approach. (Blanchot 1999: 359)

This image of *transferral* from author to page to reader will become
very important in the discussion of Coetzee's chapter on the problem
of evil in 'The Ethics of Embodiment', but here also, the idea interacts
with the book's internal (anti)argument for the co-presence of critical
and creative writing. The valley between slopes (q.v. p.44), the middle
voice – these metaphors speak of a tension of between-ness. Throughout Coetzee's work, and hopefully echoed in the interactions of this
book, runs a theme of stillness within movement. *Transferral* is occurring as a movement from author to page, to a text's implied reader, to
actual reader, yet all this movement is contained and still, happening
all at once through an overarching self-awareness of author, text and
reader. This is the reason for the repeated term 'excruciating moment'
– the moment of putting pen to paper is not referred to as an origin, a
traceable and finite point in time. Rather, the moment is available
throughout a text, containing it and undoing it in an atemporal space.

Elizabeth Costello*'s Postscript – the subject of the next chapter
of this book – reads like a chase-sequence. Here, the writing-act has
become excruciating as Lady Chandos and her muted husband pursue,
fruitlessly, those words which might fit their revelatory sensation. At
each new metaphor – shields of crystal, a wayfarer in a mill, glistening
dryads, the inner eye, soldiers on parade, a mason building a wall –
Elizabeth Chandos experiences a shudder, a literal shudder in the rup-
tured bracketed text. Is this a shudder against the poststructuralist
tenet of "Speech is no longer simply the expression of what, without
it, would *already* be an object, caught again in its primordial purity:
speech *constitutes* the object and is a concrete juridical condition of
truth" (Derrida 1978: 76)? Does Lady Chandos's despair erupt from a
deep rejection of Derrida's, Baudrillard's and other postmodern theorists' denial of reality as a site to which representations of the real can
be compared? In an interview with David Attwell, Coetzee expresses
a melancholy, if ironic, regret at the fate of postmodern writers. They
are:

> Like children shut in a playroom, the room of textual play, look-
> ing out wistfully through the bars at the enticing world of the
> grownups, one that we have been instructed to think of as the
> mere phantasmal world of *realism* but that we stubbornly can't
> help thinking of as the *real*. (Coetzee 1992: 63)

Coetzee's fiction and criticism attests to his background in mathemat-
ics, computer programming and linguistics. The adjective most frequently used by commentators to describe his writing style is *sparse*,
with *severe* a close second. The postmodern characteristics of prolif-
eration and play, as demonstrated in the work of perhaps Salman
Rushdie, John Barth or Thomas Pynchon, are absent, even negated, in
Coetzee's work. His sentences are stripped back, bare, short and de-
ceptively plain. However, it becomes clear from reading any one of
Coetzee's novels that textual play is highly apparent in his work, even
if it keeps a straight face and remains plainly saddened by its play-
room.

'I have beliefs but I do not believe in them'
In an attempt to provide a framework for reading this book, I want to
explicate the relationship between the creative and critical work, and
investigate how the interface between the two also contributes to the
methodological aims of the book as a whole. I will also discuss the
ways in which this book may be 'irregular' in the way it intends to
present theoretical, critical discussion.

First of all, there are two distinct kinds of creative writing
within this book, one being the collection of 'straight' short fiction,
which includes the stories 'Her Man and She,' 'The Nature of It,'
'Museum' and so on. The other kind of creative works are the 'Elizabeth' pieces – third person autobiography – which are less formally
partitioned from the literary criticism. In almost all cases, the creative
work has been written after, and instigated by, the themes of the criticism and not the other way around.

The placement of the creative works within the book has been
made with care. Because the discussion itself, in relation to the post-
2003 works of J. M. Coetzee, addresses the question of connections,
both similarities and differences, between critical and creative writing,
I have chosen to interleave the two rather than organise them as distinct components. Just as Elizabeth Costello, the principal character of
both *Elizabeth Costello* and *Slow Man*, presents both highly developed

arguments, and the stylized dialogue and presence of a fictional being, so too this study opts to present the critical and the creative occurring, if not within, then nearby each other, enacting my argument that the division between the two is not so bold and final as it may sometimes appear.

The pieces of short fiction within this book are stories which explore various themes of the literary analysis, transposed to a fictional world. 'The Nature of It,' for example, is a story about a judge who has taken up crime-writing, but finds himself hovering between memory and imagination when one of his characters begins to haunt his real life. The story follows a section on 'The Ethics of Embodiment,' which deals with Coetzee's exploration of the nature of authorial embodiment in *Elizabeth Costello*. One of the conclusions reached in the critical section is that embodying another, whether animal or human, 'good' or 'evil', is less a process of emptying the self than of expanding the self to a point where One and the Other may achieve a distance, like metaphor, from which to view each other. 'The Nature of It,' attempts to examine this conclusion in the character of Garrett, who feels such affinity with strangers that: "[he] could gather them up like chicks they are so familiar," and realises, as he sits at his desk trying to fill the blank screen, "*We are all the same*, he remembers thinking, and now revises, *I make everyone the same, they are all me*." In 'The Ethics of Embodiment' the book reaches a point from which to examine the practice of writing, the transferral from hand to pen to paper, as well as examining the way embodiment begins to break down the formal divisions between critical and creative writing. It seemed appropriate, then, to cluster the majority of the formal short fiction here, as 'practised' concept.

It has been an interesting process to move from critical ideas to creative writing. In most of my academic experience I have been operating the other way around, from a given creative text, fiction or poetry, to a critical analysis. It is also, perhaps, the way Coetzee has worked in writing his latest books of fiction, which refer most deliberately to philosophical and critical ideas. As Coetzee points out very quickly in Lesson One of Elizabeth Costello, 'Realism,' the difficulty is in fastening an idea to a character without making them appear a puppet or a mouthpiece: "The notion of *embodying* turns out to be pivotal. In such debates ideas do not and indeed cannot float free: they are tied to the speakers by whom they are enounced" (Coetzee 2003a:

9). I cannot say whether I have been successful in this process of embodying, indeed I am sure it has failed at times, but another process at
work in both Coetzee's and my own fiction may help to exonerate
such failures. This process is one of self- or author-awareness. Coetzee's texts, even in their most lonely places – consider Michael K
alone in his cave, still as a rock – always retain an awareness of the
author, and the author's sometimes uneasy relationship with character.
Rather than this awareness 'breaking' the fictive world, it is my argument – an argument which I hope is both observed and applied – that
the sincerity of embodiment adds further resonance to each fictional
character, including the author-character herself.

     The autobiographical 'Elizabeth' pieces serve as links or mid-
dle ground between the literary criticism and the pieces of short fiction. They often appear immediately before or after sections of more
formal theoretical writing and engage with the presented arguments
through the memories and experiences of the character 'Elizabeth,'
who reads Coetzee's books, and whose lifestyle and worldview are
altered as a result. Immediately following this section, for instance, is
an 'Elizabeth' piece which responds to ideas about the critical-creative
nexus presented both in this book and in Coetzee's latest novels. It
aims to express the problem of categorising some writing as either
'critical' or 'creative'.

The voice of the literary critic

The literary criticism in this book is itself perhaps not presented in the
regular way. I set out to write the kind of book that I myself would
enjoy reading, and realise that this may remove the book from being
eligible as 'competitive' in the field of contemporary literary theory.
Competitive in more than one sense; it does not, and never makes any
attempt to, 'compete' – as in a race or a sport – with those other perspectives on theoretical and philosophical issues which it cites. It
rather presents these other perspectives because they facilitate the continuing of an idea along its road. A large part of writing a book is saying 'no' to various paradigms and texts which are certainly accessible
and probably also interesting and relevant, but for which there is simply not enough time or room to explore. Those ideas then, to which
this book says 'yes,' – for example textual and linguistic analysis, the
author-character relationship, the concept of re-reading, the ethics of
embodiment, self-awareness – which many other people have written

about, and are still writing about, travel along with the book, and hopefully enrich it.

One of my aims as I wrote the sections of literary criticism in this book was to write about interesting ideas in a way which paralleled those forms of narrative the ideas drew from. In other words, the aim was to write about theory so that the discussion took on the form of a good narrative – so that it travelled, encountered divergences, and did not end with all its questions wrapped and finished. The overriding viewpoint behind this kind of methodology returns again to the idea of embodiment: an idea or philosophy does not, cannot, 'float free', but is tied to the idiosyncrasies, divergences, and subjective 'travel' of its speaker or writer. Texts produced under this paradigm might, then, exist as hybrids between fiction and theory. Books like Coetzee's *Elizabeth Costello* and *Diary of a Bad Year* which are indisputably difficult to read, are oddly structured, contain arguments that are easily, in fact demonstrably, untenable, and which end sourly, contain that thing – a seam of personal scrutiny, even distress – that compel readers' down from (detached) argument to the (attached) lips of the person speaking. Critics have accused Coetzee of slyly answering his own critics with his Elizabeth Costello works – pointing out their shortcomings internally before they can be pointed out elsewhere. For me this is not an indication of the books' weakness, or of their failure to stand 'on their own' without needing recourse to self-analysis; rather, I view it as a brave, unique and authentic inscription of the person of the author upon his writing. As so many of Coetzee's pained author-figures attest, the best writing is also a sacrifice. Although there may be other books within Coetzee's oeuvre which are 'better,' having more successfully been 'texts' – finely crafted, intelligent, moving, rounded – the two recent Elizabeth Costello works, as well as *Diary of a Bad Year,* make it known that they are indebted to a moment of sacrifice when pen gained page.

Although I do not presume that this book is unique or even brave, I do agree with Anya, who has provided this section with its epigraph, that a 'know-it-all tone' really turns people off and that there must be a better, or at least alternative way. In a recent article on a new poetics for the PhD, Kevin Brophy discusses the nature of PhD writing, describing the process of drafting as a conversation between writer and reader – the writer having the opportunity to act as both:

> The challenge and opportunity for the writer is to create a text out
> of this exchange between the self as writer and the self as reader,
> one which records the exchange in a kind of writing that is pro-
> ductive, intelligent, testing, pre-emptive and exploratory. The ex-
> pectation on the part of the reader is that the document will ad-
> dress many of the possible responses, objections and reactions go-
> ing through the reader's mind as the document is read. (Brophy
> 2007)

The difficult question, of course, is how much of this pre-written conversation of arguments and objections should be included in the discussion, and at what point, if any, should this exchange bow out
gracefully and allow one thread of argument to remain, perhaps to triumph, should we see the exchange as a competitive one. Coetzee's
Elizabeth Costello books are also built out of these sorts of exchanges.
Whatever statements Costello makes, whatever beliefs she may ascribe to, they always encounter an objection, a rejoinder. It may come
from her audience, from her family, from her characters, and indeed
from herself; "I have beliefs but I do not believe in them," she says.
What remains, in a statement such as this, whose objects and verbs
negate each other, is the subject, 'I', which stands behind, and embodies, the arguments and counter-arguments, the statements and their
consequent falling down.

*

"If I began an essay enclosed in quotation marks, for instance, a message to the reader is signalled, and the signal is questioned: 'who is the
speaker?' 'can the author still hold responsibility for arguments which
are enclosed in quotation marks?' 'to what extent is this playful or
ironic?' 'how do I read this?'

"However, rather than being confounded by such questions, rather
than taking offence to the 'distance' from which the essayist might be
seen to be holding the essay – at arm's length as it were – could we
not redirect our attention to the confoundedness, the irony, of essays
not so enclosed in quotation marks?

"The quotation mark indicates another person, whose mouth is opening somewhere, at some place, at some point in time, usually with

some other person, or group of persons, who act as listener or conversant or audience.

"In other words, the quotation mark situates. It indicates specificity. The question of *who* is being specified – author or someone else – and further whether the essay should be viewed as 'real' or 'fictive', are the very questions an essay in quotation marks would like to undermine as being, to some extent, beside the point.

"What, then, does an essay without quotation mark do? It remains unsituated, non-specific. It does not come from a certain open mouth, within a place with walls as such, in front of a listener like this.

"Can it then be read as though spoken by anyone, at any time, in any place, and listened to by everyone, and interpreted in every way? Yes, for this is how it was meant to be read.

"For the essay without quotation mark, the person writing or speaking, where she sits, or stands, to whom she delivers her essay, and all the things that have brought her to this place at this time are unimportant. The words she erased and rewrote are unimportant. The doubts she has about the thread of her argument are unimportant, and hidden. What remains, and is considered important, is the idea being expounded.

"Certainly, some essayists – Nietzsche for example, or Adorno – have been noted almost as much for the style – abrupt, convoluted – as the content of their essays. A distinctive style, in a sense, situates an essay, just as a quotation mark does (or gives the impression it will eventually), in that it locates the essay as emanating from a particular person who writes in a particular (quirky) way. The ideas, however, about which they write do not often site the author in the same way. In fact, even when their ideas are about the disintegration of universal truth (which they often seem to be), still the ideas are received as though they had been floating in the air and happened to be plucked down by this author – what was his name again, flick back to the title page, oh yes such-and-such.

"In other words the ideas are regularly given an authority which exists apart from the person who wrote them down.

"The essay, if it contains or is bestowed this authority, is allowed to stand on its own, sometimes for decades to come. The author's name may then become synonymous with the essay.

"Even if, in the meantime, the author ages, changes their view completely, has three sons, commits a crime, falls over in the bathtub, breaks a hip, and dies.

"All of this because the author is situationless. Their words, without quotation marks, are *originals*. Only later, when a sound-byte is required by some student or commentator as representative of the ideas of such-and-such, are the words placed carefully between regulatory quotation marks. 'I didn't write these words,' say the quotation marks, 'but I might as well have since they now belong to my essay and serve to further the ideas therein.'

"If I were, then, to begin an essay in quotation marks, and those various uncomfortable signals transmitted to the reader, what would it do to the way we usually read? Rather than figuring a name – such-and-such – alongside, or bound with, its espoused idea – such-and-suchism – a reader might find themselves entering the moment of the text as it is produced. They might be able to wander around a room, watch the faces of an audience, hear the voice and even imagine the inner misgivings of an author. The essay would then become something that happened at one point, *an event*, rather than, perhaps, a truth, which is always happening."

Elizabeth released a breath and nodded slightly, to let her listeners know, since they obviously were not sure, that she had finished. A smattering of applause, and a couple of encouraging smiles – the sort of encouraging smiles that made her feel very young. People raised their hands to ask questions, which she answered, but later could remember nothing of her response.

Riding the tram home Elizabeth could not quite place how she felt. Ridiculous, on the one hand, but relieved, but a little exultant. And that old feeling too, of falling backwards, back into her quiet self after simulating the image of a talkative, authoritative, composed young scholar. Of course, the falling back was not so hard or far now. Her imagined selves were beginning to align.

A young man with protruding teeth boarded the tram and sat next to her, smiling, and told her he had woken up at six-thirty to make it into the city in time for his computer skills training course, which he had completed before but had been told by his new employer that he must take it again, and the new uniform he had been issued was eighty percent synthetic, only twenty percent natural materials, and it made his skin break out, see, and would she mind if he had some water from that bottle she had, it's just he needed two litres a day at least.

'Thank you,' he said and handed the bottle.

'You keep it,' Elizabeth said, and smiled in a friendly, but not over-friendly, way.

*

The critical landscape
Since the publication of *Elizabeth Costello* criticism and commentary on Coetzee's work has shifted its focus substantially, mirroring the shift in the novels themselves.

Reviews of *Costello* have proven to be an interesting gauge, and useful to my analysis in terms of what they have chosen to focus on as the 'point' of Coetzee's book. Not surprisingly, many reviewers concentrated on the extremity and controversial nature of Costello's lectures. Something which is quoted in almost every review is Costello's analogy, in 'The Philosophers and the Animals,' between the mass killing of Hitler's holocaust and the mass killing of animals in slaughterhouses:

> Let me say it openly: we are surrounded by an enterprise of degradation, cruelty and killing which rivals anything that the Third Reich was capable of, indeed dwarfs it, in that ours is an enterprise without end, self-regenerating, bringing rabbits, rats, poultry, livestock ceaselessly into the world for the purpose of killing them. (Coetzee 2003a: 65)

There is a genuine feeling of bewilderment amongst reviewers as they tackle this passage and its context. Phrases like "oblique commentary," "puzzling lesson" and "ambiguous morality," from Jennifer Schuessler's review in the *Boston Globe* are common (Schuessler 2003). Yardley's damning review repeatedly uses the word 'mystery': "Precisely what Coetzee is trying to say in [the lectures] may be clear to him but is often a mystery to the reader," and "why he did not publish them as a collection of his nonfiction, rather than fobbing them off as a work of fiction, is a mystery he alone can solve" (Yardley 2003). Andrew Riemer's review in the *Sydney Morning Herald* also focuses on Costello's ambiguous nature: "For Elizabeth Costello, there are no certainties; she does not know whether she believes what she thinks she believes. Everything is provisional, constantly challenged by doubt, by gnawing scepticism" (Riemer 2003). David Lodge, in *The New York Review of Books*, sums up: "Not surprisingly most of the commentators felt somewhat stymied by Coetzee's meta-lectures" (Lodge 2003).

Costello and her arguments' vulnerability is traced by James Wood, a colleague of Coetzee's at the Dostoevsky conference where Coetzee delivered his 'Problem of Evil' lecture. In his thoughtful article Wood writes, "Literary argumentation must take literary form. But this in turn means that ideas cannot be won, that they are vulnerable" (Wood 2003). Although some commentators discuss Costello's rejection of philosophical reasoning in favour of imagination and 'the heart', few consider this most important observation. Marjorie Garber, in her response to Coetzee's original Tanner lectures, touches upon the issue at the end of her essay. She writes:

> Poetry makes nothing happen, W. H. Auden once wrote…What has poetry to offer, what has language to offer, by way of solace, except analogy, except the art of language? In these two elegant lectures we thought John Coetzee was talking about animals. Could it be, however, that all along he was really asking, 'What is the value of literature?' (Garber in Coetzee 1999b: 84)

Apart from literature on *Elizabeth Costello* itself, Coetzee's novels from 1974's *Dusklands* to 2002's *Youth* and their corresponding critical literature provide a body of support for my study of Coetzee's case for the value of literature. Although I will be focussing on those novels which have a particular concern for the author-character

(*Age of Iron, Master of Petersburg, Foe*) all of Coetzee's works are demonstrations, both realist and reflexive, of the author divided. Teresa Dovey's weighty study, *The Novels of J. M. Coetzee: Lacanian Allegories*, uses Lacan's models of the subject to negotiate Coetzee's self-discourse in his novels: "The content of Coetzee's novels becomes the performance itself, as the traditional themes and the theme of the Lacanian subject intersect to produce allegories of the narrating self" (Dovey 1988: 14). Dovey's book, based on her earlier doctoral thesis, stands out as a study which uses an overarching psychoanalytic and narratological premise to which Coetzee's novels are, variously, subjected. Other critical studies such as Dominic Head's *J. M. Coetzee*, part of a Cambridge series on African and Caribbean literature, have no such overarching reading in their chapter-length analyses of each novel to date. Coetzee's South African-ness is, in fact, the binding argument, as the faintly new historicist 'Chronology' displays; here various political junctures are interspersed with biographical points of interest (Head 1997: xiv-xvi). The same is true of almost all substantial critical analyses through the 1990s: Gallagher's 1991 *A Story of South Africa: J. M. Coetzee's Fiction in Context*, Atwell's 1993 *J. M. Coetzee: South Africa and the Politics of Writing*, Kossew's 1996 *Pen and Power: a Post-Colonial Reading of J. M. Coetzee and André Brink* and Helgesson's 1999 *Sports of Culture: Writing the Resistant Subject in South Africa*. Coetzee himself may indicate a subtle weariness with the narrowness of this critical lens when he has Elizabeth Costello's son express concern that "his mother not be treated as a Mickey Mouse post-colonial writer" (2003a: 9).

From 2003 onwards, however, driven both by the appearance of Costello – her crotchety nature as much as her scandalous ideas – and by Coetzee's physical removal from his country of birth to Australia, a flurry of commentary has dramatically shifted its focus from culture and postcolonialism to philosophy and ethics. Derek Attridge's 2004 *J. M. Coetzee and the Ethics of Reading: Literature in the Event*, without overlooking the South African dimension of his fiction, treats Coetzee as a writer who raises questions of central importance to current debates both within literary studies and more widely in the ethical arena. Implicit throughout the book is Attridge's view that literature, more than philosophy, politics, or even religion, does singular justice to our ethical impulses and acts. Stephen Mulhall's 2008 *The Wounded Animal: J. M. Coetzee and the Difficulty of Reality in Lit-*

erature and Philosophy also examines Coetzee's writings about Costello, and the ways in which philosophers have responded to them. Carrol Clarkson's 2009 *J. M. Coetzee: Countervoices* addresses the interaction between Coetzee's fiction and his critical writing, exploring the author's participation in, and contribution to, contemporary literary-philosophical debates. *J. M. Coetzee and Ethics: Philosophical Perspectives on Literature,* edited by Anton Leist and Peter Singer in 2010, explores Coetzee's approach to ethical theory and philosophy and pays particular attention to his novels' representation of the human-animal relationship. J. C. Kannemeyer's comprehensive 2012 biography *J. M. Coetzee: A life in writing*, as the title suggests, structures itself around the publication of Coetzee's books, enacting Coetzee's words to David Attwell, "All autobiography is storytelling, all writing is autobiography" (Coetzee 1992: 391).

Of the wealth of journal articles on Coetzee's novels I have tried to be selective, finding those commentaries which focus, broadly, on Coetzee's various uses and observations of language to be the most helpful for my perspective. Michael Marais's excellent 'Ethics, Engagement, and Change…' is an example of an article which asks a question of Coetzee's engagement with history by both interrogating his novels and drawing upon the philosophies of writers like Blanchot and Emmanuel Levinas (Marais 2000).

Reading Coetzee, then, is situated in excellent company for a discussion of the value of literature and the interrogation of the literature-philosophy divide as represented in Coetzee's recent works. Taking its lead directly from Coetzee's books, however, this work also presents its analysis in hybrid form: I am not only observing, but participating in the creative process. I attempt to engage not only the analytical, disembodied voice of the critic (like Costello's voice at the podium of the lecture theatre), but also the personal, decidedly embodied voice of the woman, the reader (like Costello's inner voice, and inner narration beyond the lectures).

In terms of the broader critical landscape which has informed the conceptual framework of this book, the essays of French theorist Maurice Blanchot are invaluable when discussing both the moment of writing – the dread and confusion that shadows this moment – and the work or value of literature. Blanchot enters these moments and issues with a precision and focus that I have not encountered elsewhere. The issue of the temporal, as will be discussed in regard to the Kafkaesque Lesson 8, is of further relevance: Blanchot, in both his fiction and criticism, enters time in a way which seems to expand it infinitely. The excruciating moment of writing, therefore, becomes a vast landscape of slopes, forked paths and convergences. Coetzee's fiction, in the same way, gives the impression of moving forward while remaining perfectly still and contained – his books, because they constantly indicate their inception, remain static even while characters are moving about, living, dying and continuing.

Michael Marais, in his essay on ethics, engagement and change in Coetzee's work, also discusses the unmistakeable connection between Coetzee's fiction and Blanchot's discourse, especially the latter's writings on the gaze of Orpheus. Marais compares Blanchot's "meditation on the impossibility of the writer's desire for the Other, that is, the impossibility of either actualizing or eliminating radical otherness" with various encounters between characters in Coetzee's fiction, such as that between Jacobus Coetzee and the Namaqua tribe in *Dusklands* (Marais 2000: 163). Blanchot's essays, as this example suggests, hinge upon paradox. As ambiguity, paradox and chiasmus hold an important place in *Elizabeth Costello* – both as 'techniques' and subjects for discussion – their place in my conceptual framework is significant.

As Blanchot himself suggests in the following passage, resorting to ambiguity as an answer is unsatisfactory:

> To say to this torment: I obey it by abandoning my written thought to oscillation, by expressing it through a code, would be to represent it as interesting me only in the mystery in which it reveals itself; however I know it more as mysterious than as familiar, neither as a key to a world which has no key, nor as an answer to the absence of a question…it is there – of that I am certain – but it is there in the dark… Ambiguity presupposes a secret that no doubt expresses itself by vanishing, but that in this vanishing allows itself to be glimpsed as a possible truth. (Blanchot 1999: 352-353)

Another famous moment of chiasmus appears in Roland Barthes's *Mythologies* in a passage regarding the demystification of objects:

> We constantly drift between the object and its demystification, powerless to render its wholeness. For if we penetrate the object,

we liberate it but we destroy it; and if we acknowledge its full
weight, we respect it, but we restore it to a state which is still
mystified. (Barthes 1972b: 159)

It is this kind of struggle which *Elizabeth Costello* – at once highly
moral and highly ambiguous – refuses to allow to lapse into a settled
paradox. "It *is* there", writes Blanchot, "but it is there in the dark".
With a rigor that again defies a general postmodernist playfulness and
delight in paradox, Coetzee's book does search out answers, and,
through the dry ironic voice of Elizabeth Costello, does offer them. A
significant part of my conceptual framework, then, involves finding a
way between accepting ambiguity as a foregone conclusion and offering concrete answers to far-from-concrete questions.

　　As will be observed through the link between the 1902 Lord
Chandos letter and *Elizabeth Costello's* Postscript, another aspect of a
conceptual framework involves a model of Literature as an unfolding
phenomenon in time. From Chandos's reliance on a realistic connection between ideas and words, to his prophetic modernist 'wheelbar-
row moment' whereby objects and words became almost independent
of one another. And thus on to Coetzee's response with the feminine
voice expounding on the postmodern unreachable Other and looking
beyond to a monstrous future. An important aspect of the voice of
Elizabeth Costello is its insistence on moving forward, using the past
to create the future.

Reading about the writing act inevitably draws one towards thinking
about the reading act. Various indistinct ideas I had regarding the spa-
tiality of a text I realised had been studied in the niche area of literary
theory known as *rereading*. Often the term is used sparsely in the bodies of work on (German) reception theory and (American) reader-
response theory, but as Matei Calinescu's book *Rereading* points out,
rather indignantly, there is hardly any significant or specific work
done on the topic of rereading texts. I came to these bodies of literature an empty canvas with Elizabeth Costello's words ringing around
my head: "The experience that writing offers, or reading…is not a
relative one, relative to the writer and the writer's capacities, relative
to the reader…Mr West, when he wrote those chapters, came in touch
with something absolute. Absolute evil" (Coetzee 2003a: 175-6). This
is, of course, a radical thing to say, or, rather, a very old-fashioned
thing to say. In this post-Barthes, post-Lyotard age Costello's com-

ment might seem ridiculous or ironic. Reception theorists such as Roman Ingarden and Wolfgang Iser who were writing in the late sixties, do not think twice about placing the reader firmly in control of the various 'potentialities' and 'concretisations' offered by any text (Holub 1984: 25-29; 83-106). Reader-response theorists Stanley Fish and Norman Holland posit a reader-active model of reading whereby both the reader's personal identity and the various codes of reading combine in the retrieval of a text's interpretation (Holland 1993: 1383). Taking something as an 'absolute' is, if even mentioned, seen as one of the dangers of logic that theorising reading could fall into.

With regard to my own reading, however, the literature offered various articulations of the process of reading which I found useful when considering the conceptual frameworks I was using. Calinescu regards the demarcation between first-time reading and re-reading as an instinctive way of solving a temporal puzzle:

> Our intuition that the essential successiveness of the first reading of a literary work can be reversed in a second reading, and that this reversal may result in a spatial consciousness of the work as a 'landscape'…a rereader might feel that a work with which he or she is already familiar is available to understanding not only as a past, remembered diachronic unfolding, but also as a present synchronic structure. (Calinescu 1993: 18)

Calinescu goes on to suggest that although using spatial metaphors (such as Proust's description of *À la recherche du temps perdu* as a cathedral) is useful in this instinctive way, the temporal aspect of reading is unavoidable, if its import is broadened. As Barthes writes: "'Rereading draws the text out of its internal chronology ("this happened *before* or *after* that") and recaptures a mythic time…rereading is no longer consumption, but play'" (Barthes 1974: 16).

The opening 'Elizabeth' section of the following chapter 'Metaphor as Contagion' reports the memory of a first-time reading (of *Disgrace*) and implicates this memory as a factor in the process of buying and reading *Elizabeth Costello*. Looking at this passage through the lens of the rereader, my aim was not so much to provide the text with a physical history, or to emphasize the coincidental fate of this book (as I first thought). Rather, the 'Elizabeth' pieces are moments of interruption and circular citation, a manhandling (and thus rereading) of the text and its place in time. As Calinescu writes, here citing T. S. Eliot, "The 'aesthetic' past, unlike the purely 'historical' past is 'altered by the present as much as the present is directed by the past.' In other words, what happens when a new work of art is created is something that happens simultaneously to all the works of art that preceded it" (Calinescu 1993: 54).[1] The various intermingled pieces in this book, in terms of my conceptual framework, are thereby meant as reverberations of each other and of *Elizabeth Costello* and of all the various works which precede and will proceed from Coetzee's book.

Coetzee's recurring blank page

Without doubt, the image of the blank page and the figure of the suffering writer are elements which Coetzee has utilised in every one of his novels to date. I suggest that they are not simply recurring themes which give structure to a political agenda, but that they form the base of his writing and philosophy. *Elizabeth Costello* and *Slow Man* are books which make Coetzee's lifelong concentration on the value of the act of writing explicit. His books are littered with motifs of the white page and the struggling storyteller, but in the figures of the ageing author Costello, the despairing Chandoses, the cripple Paul Rayment, the motif-cycle reaches a defining point.

In *Waiting for the Barbarians*, Coetzee's 1980 novel, the Magistrate begins a new document, a different one from his many years of government files and records of the strange language of the ancient barbarians, husks of which he has dug up from the outskirts of the settlement.

> What the second document is to be I do not yet know. A testament? A memoir? A confession? A history of thirty years on the frontier? All that day I sit in a trance at my desk staring at the empty white paper, waiting for words to come. A second day passes in the same way. On the third day I surrender, put the paper back in the drawer, and make preparations to leave. It seems appropriate that a man who does not know what to do with the woman in his bed should not know what to write. (Coetzee 1980: 57-8)

---

[1] Calinescu is referring here to T. S. Eliot's 1919 essay 'Tradition and the Individual Talent' in Frank Kermode (ed.) 1975 *Selected Prose*. New York: Harcourt Brace.

This sense of impotence at the inability to tell one's story, or even to choose from the possibilities of the white paper, is heard again in 1983's *Life and Times of Michael K*, a book which could be described as a study in silence and solitude. Michael is asked time and again for his story, but finds he always gives the wrong one: "Always, when he tried to explain himself to himself, there remained a gap, a hole, a darkness before which his understanding baulked, into which it was useless to pour words. The words were eaten up, the gap remained. His was always a story with a hole in it: a wrong story, always wrong" (Coetzee 1983: 150-1). When confronted for harbouring the enemy at his isolated farmhouse and pumpkin patch, Michael realises how dangerous it is to be without a story:

> The soldier who was holding K gripped the nape of his neck between thumb and forefinger and guided him down till he was kneeling, till his face was touching the earth. 'You heard what the officer said,' he said, 'so tell me. Tell me your story.' He flicked the beret away and pressed K's face hard into the earth. With nose and lips squashed flat, K tasted damp soil. He sighed. They lifted him and held him up. He did not open his eyes. 'So tell us about your friends,' the soldier said. K shook his head. He was hit a terrific blow in the pit of the stomach and fainted. (Coetzee 1983: 168)

Earlier in the book Michael describes himself as "the stony ground", (65) a metaphor which recalls Pierre Macherey's image of "a ground on which a story traces a figure...a *certain absence*, without which it would not exist...for in order to say anything, there are other things *which must not be said*" (Macherey 1978: 85). Again, Coetzee is running along the edge of irony with his delicate, impeccable story of a man silenced to it.

Age of Iron, which appeared in 1990, is a long letter from a mother living in iron-hardened South Africa to her daughter who has escaped to North America. Again, we are faced with the blank page: "I was sitting up in bed, gloves on my hands, the writing pad on my knees. For half an hour I had sat with the page blank before me." Again, the reader is shown the fraught process of putting pen to paper, "I cannot take the pills and go on with the writing. So without pain no writing: a new and terrible rule" (Coetzee 1990: 174-5). And again, the reader is made agonizingly aware that this book in their hands is the product of someone's suffering, someone's sick, pained, shaking hand making its way across the white space.

Nowhere is this impression more blatantly affirmed than in 1994's *The Master of Petersburg,* Coetzee's ode to Fyodor Dosto-evsky. As Dostoevsky goes through the letters and stories his adopted son Pavel has left behind after dying violently due to his Bolshevik associations, he is desperate for the lost youth to know where his writ-ing comes from: "There is something overwhelmingly important he wants to say that the boy will now never be able to hear. If you are blessed with the power to write, he wants to say, bear in mind the source of that power. You write *because* your childhood was lonely, *because* you were not loved" (Coetzee 1994: 152). Suffering and infi-delity as the source of writing is the theme upon which the book, with brutal and exacting force, finishes itself: "He has betrayed every-one...It seems to him a great price to pay. *They pay him lots of money for writing books*, said the child, repeating the dead child. What they failed to say was that he had to give up his soul in return" (250). Again, as with the Chandoses' cries for salvation, there is so much at stake for Fyodor between the divides of writing: "But he knows too that as long as he tries by cunning to distinguish things that are things from things that are signs he will not be saved" (83).

In Coetzee's 1999 novel *Disgrace* David Lurie postpones his opera about the life of Byron for fear of further devaluing himself: "He has, if truth be told, been putting it off for months: the moment when he must face the blank page, strike the first note, see what he is worth" (Coetzee 1999a: 121). The figure of the impotent artist is brought up again in a not quite sincere way in *Youth*, the story of a young man who longs to suffer enough to be able to write like the modernist artists he most admires, Ezra Pound, T. S. Eliot, Ford Madox Ford, but who instead finds himself living a life of unbearable banality as a computer programmer. His blank page is therefore a source of intense frustration: "He hates these confrontations with the blank page, hates them to the extent of beginning to avoid them" (Co-etzee 2002: 166).

This study of *Elizabeth Costello* and *Slow Man* is important for providing a conceptual framework for a rereading of Coetzee's previous body of literature. Whereas the majority of criticism on Co-etzee's work still deals with, as Teresa Dovey puts it, 'the South Afri-can situation,' or brackets it as postcolonial literature, this study takes as its focal point the crucial questions Coetzee raises concerning the writing-act and the value of literature.

The written is always a compromise

The following chapter examines the Postscript of *Elizabeth Costello*, a letter written from what seems to be a nadir of suffering and confusion, Coetzee is making reference not only to the suffering of the writer, to the excruciating moment of putting pen to paper when surrounded by the two extremes of silence, but also to the falsity of this suffering, the figurativeness of it, the 'metaphor-icity' of it. Costello herself describes this writer-figure, with some amount of scorn in Lesson 8: "She sees herself, a stick-like figure on a public bench in a patch of sunlight scribbling away at her task, a task never to be completed. *God save me!* she whispers to herself. *Too literary, too literary! I must get out of here before I die!*" (Coetzee 2003a: 215). The image mirrors Blanchot's idea of the writer trapped in paradox: "The writer finds himself in this more and more comical condition – of having nothing to write, of having no means of writing it, and of being forced by an extreme necessity to keep writing it" (Blanchot 1999: 345).

It has been suggested, for instance by Jonathan Yardley in the Washington Post, that the only reason Coetzee was able to publish this book is because he is J. M. Coetzee: "His trophy case is crammed with rave reviews and prizes, including most recently a Nobel Prize and, in advance of that, a brace of Bookers...*Elizabeth Costello* is an exercise in the higher self-indulgence" (Yardley 2003). In one way this is derogatory – implying that Coetzee is now in a position to write anything at all, and no matter how strange, unreadable, insulting or conceited it is, it will be published regardless. In another way, however, the statement rings with a different kind of credibility. Perhaps it is true that the only reason Coetzee feels himself to be in a position to present lectures using a fictional context and character is because he is John Maxwell Coetzee, double-Booker winner and Nobel winner. Perhaps the only reason he published this book which places the status of the literary celebrity into question, which questions the value of literature as a whole, is because he is J. M. Coetzee, famous for his reclusiveness, adamant vegetarianism and refusal to give interviews. Elizabeth Costello herself, who is also accused (by her son among others) of riding out old hobby-horses simply because she now can,

wonders if she is being self-indulgent by not being 'the writer' expected of her. And not only simply 'the writer,' but the feminist, colo-
nial writer of *The House on Eccles Street*. She is constantly disap-
pointing people: "*She has let us down*, they will say. *Elizabeth
Costello has turned into old Mother Grundy*" (Coetzee 2003a: 168).

What is clear from reading this Postscript and Hofmannsthal's
forerunner, is that, like the statue of the Venus de Milo, writing looks
solid to the touch, timeless, sincere, pure and familiar. But, like the
Venus de Milo, the written is always a compromise – unfinished,
making constant reference to *how it was meant to be*. This makes the
act of writing a strange gesture, for if all speaking falls short, then
why all these words?

Metaphor as Contagion:
On the Postscript of *Elizabeth Costello*

*Any banal sentence attests to the despair that exists in the depths of
language.*
Maurice Blanchot

Elizabeth Costello as Postscript to Coetzee's oeuvre

Elizabeth Costello is, on its own, an important book of its time. In
2003 J. M. Coetzee was perhaps the most celebrated author writing in
English for the previous thirty years. Arriving as it did shortly after
the award of a Nobel Prize for Literature, perhaps at the zenith of his
contemporary influence, the book commanded a global audience of
critics and readers.

Coetzee, moreover, produced a book which baffled his critics and
fans, as typified in the title of one review: 'It's very novel, but is it
actually a novel?' In comparison to his other recent novels like *Disgrace* and the autobiographical *Youth* and *Boyhood*, *Elizabeth
Costello* is conspicuously different – it seems to be driven by ideas
rather than plot or character. If it could be viewed as the third in a
chronological trilogy of autobiography, then it is certainly much more
coy and impersonal than the preceding two. In comparison to Coetzee's other theoretical writing, *Elizabeth Costello* also travels in a new
direction. Even when some of the content is similar, as with his 1995
essay on animal slaughtering, 'Meat Country' (Coetzee 1995), the
'animal' chapters in *Costello* are imbued with such a sense of the personal against the backdrop of Costello's 'seal-trainer' son and disdain-
ful daughter-in-law, that one does not know quite how to think about
this grandmother's philosophies.

Another striking aspect of this book when compared to Coetzee's previous work is its sense of self-deprecation – its attention to
the process of altering one's views, ardently held in youth, over time.

In this sense the book is almost confessional. In Lesson 6, 'The Problem of Evil,' when Costello is mulling over her lecture 'Witness, Silence and Censorship,' she reflects on the way her standard set of principles is undergoing a 'quiet' change:

> The routine censorship paper is liberal in its ideas, with perhaps a touch of the *Kulturpessimismus* that has marked her thinking of late: the civilization of the West is based on belief in unlimited and illimitable endeavour, it is too late for us to do anything about that, we must simply hold on tight and go wherever the ride takes us. It is on the subject of the illimitable that her opinions seem to be undergoing a quiet change…Specifically, she is no longer sure that people are always improved by what they read. (Coetzee 2003a: 160)

If one knows Coetzee's work, it is impossible to read the above section of the novel without thinking of his 1996 book, *Giving Offense: Essays on Censorship*, which, although interrogating the way in which giving and taking offence becomes a matter of power and politics, does not delve so far, as *Elizabeth Costello* does, into the question of the good of literature – let alone reach the conclusion that putting forth an argument for the censorship of obscenity is justified. *Elizabeth Costello* seems in fact to be the kind of authoritative book an author would write late in their career, or at least once their 'name' has been established. If a reader approached the writings of Coetzee using this book as their entry, it is doubtful they would have an understanding of what Coetzee is most famous and celebrated for – namely his austere rendering of character and narrative. *Elizabeth Costello* makes overt reference not only to Coetzee's previous books, but also to his own life as a 'touring' speech-maker and award-receiver. A study of this book, then, is important for its unusually reflective, self-doubting and seemingly old-fashioned presentation of moral systems, and as a re-opening of Coetzee's previous books – a reflection on the ideas and the metamorphoses contained in them.

When Coetzee's novel, *Slow Man*, was published in September 2005, the reappearance of the Elizabeth Costello character brought about a shift, or perhaps enlargement, of emphasis in this study. Now here were *two* books which utilized this perplexing author-figure/ doppelgänger, two sets of public reaction, particularly circulating around Booker prize commentary. The fact that, for the first time, Coetzee had carried a character from one novel into a second was enough to question again her introduction and her, perhaps exasperating, persistence. The link between author and character became even more compelling; it was as though Coetzee couldn't get rid of (or perhaps 'take care of') Costello, or was it the other way around? In any case, *Slow Man* is a disquieting, highly original novel which addresses again those elemental questions of the writer: why write? why write about *this*? from where do characters come? what is the relationship between writer and character? how much of oneself can/should be revealed before a work of fiction becomes something else? Thus *Slow Man* became another central work to which this book referred.

*

Elizabeth was in the middle of reading a new book by J. M. Coetzee. She thought of this author as John Maxwell Coetzee, South African writer now living part-time in her home town of Adelaide, double-Booker Prize winner, Nobel-prize winner, semi-recluse, author of *Disgrace*. This was the sum of her knowledge of the author. She had read *Disgrace* the year before, immediately after reading Jonathan Franzen's *The Corrections,* and so her impression of the book was one of a distinctly un-American, slightly wan, slow-moving, firmly structured novel involving academia, violence and dogs. She had read the last half of *Disgrace* while in bed doubled over with menstrual pain and nausea in a kind of sleepless empty-stomached dream. Her memory of the scenes in the veterinary clinic and the dog dumping-ground were, therefore, particularly pungent in her mind, mouth and throat. *Those dogs*, she thought whenever the book came to mind, *those burning redemptive dogs.*

The book she was reading now had caught her eye in the new release section of a bookstore. Normally she didn't buy new hardcover books unless it was a particularly favourite author or special occasion, and the first thing she looked at when she picked up this one was the price sticker on the back. The book cost $32.95. It seemed costly for such a slim volume. Elizabeth did some calculations in her head, a series of subtractions from the hundred dollars a week she received from study allowance. She then remembered she would be receiving an extra sixty dollars the next day for some past tutoring work.

She began reading the back cover of the book which listed complimentary quotes from newspapers like the *Guardian*, the *Ob-*

server and the *Sunday Telegraph*. Michelle de Kretser had written in the *Weekend Australian* "Coetzee is the vivisectionist of the human condition." Elizabeth began to think that she would definitely buy this book. Her eyes drifted to the top of the page where it said "Praise for *Disgrace*". *Damn,* she thought, *why do they always do that?* She then realised that because the book was brand new, there was probably no praise for it yet.

She opened the front cover of the book and read the blurb on the inside dust-jacket. The last line read, "J. M. Coetzee's latest work of fiction offers us a profound and delicate vision of literary celebrity, artistry and the private life of the mind." *An academic book*, thought Elizabeth, *Perhaps a book about Coetzee himself.* There were two more things to look at. The contents page interested her greatly. The chapters were called 'Lessons'; there were eight lessons followed by a Postscript. The lessons had titles like 'Realism,' 'The Problem of Evil,' and 'The Humanities in Africa'. *A moral book*, Elizabeth thought, *A postmodern self-consciously literary book.* She turned to the first page and read "There is first of all the problem of the opening, namely, how to get us from where we are, which is, as yet, nowhere, to the far bank. It is a simple bridging problem, a problem of knocking together a bridge".

Elizabeth was captivated. She bought the book and tried to convince herself it was because of the book's author, its intriguing blurb, its unique contents page, its exquisite first line, and not because she shared her name with the title and central character of the book, *Elizabeth Costello*.

*

Lord Chandos's total renunciation of literary activity

The Postscript of *Elizabeth Costello*, the far bank as it were, is a letter written by yet another Elizabeth, this time Lady Elizabeth Chandos, wife of Lord Philip Chandos. Lord Chandos was the author of a fictional letter addressed to Sir Francis Bacon and dated 1603. The letter was actually written by Hugo von Hofmannsthal and originally published in German in 1902. Coetzee's Lady Chandos letter is also addressed to Sir Francis Bacon and is written as a result of her husband's letter having "come under my sight" (Coetzee 2003a: 227).

Hofmannsthal's original Lord Chandos letter is, by way of introduction, "an apology to his friend for his total renunciation of literary activity" (Hofmannsthal 1986: 11). Lord Chandos has found himself in the unenviable situation of having "utterly lost [his] ability to think or speak coherently about anything at all" (19). He describes this situation in two ways, the first being his increasing sense of help-lessness, isolation and silence in the face of language, the second his fervent search for revelation in the form of a higher or other language. The former situation is illustrated by a series of losses; departures from Chandos's former "delirious days" when he wrote prolifically and joyously, "creating poetry and truth together, a play of eternal forces, a thing as glorious as music or algebra" (15). In those days Chandos could discern no difference between the intellectual and the physical, finding them no more contradictory than "the life of Court and that of animals, than art and non-art, or than solitude and society" (17). In short Chandos felt a vast unity in all creation and himself at the centre. There was no difference, is the inference, between the natural world and the written world, between milk and the metaphor of milk (17).

Gradually, however, Chandos finds that the words he once used to talk about abstract concepts begin to turn "to dust in my mouth like decaying mushrooms" (19). On the verge of berating his little daughter for lying, he finds himself rendered speechless as the concepts of truth-telling and integrity begin to blur in front of his eyes until he can no longer see or reach them at all. He describes the situation as a succession of breakages and ruptures: "Everything fell into fragments for me, the fragments into further fragments, until it seemed impossible to contain anything at all within a single concept" (21). He also uses the image of magnification to express the way in which concepts became enlarged to the point of being invisible: "Just as I once saw a bit of skin of my little finger in a magnifying glass, and found it to resemble a huge field full of ridges and hollows, so it was for me now" (21). Where previously he felt the world and its mysteries to be a "single sublime allegory" (18) Chandos now feels the world breaking apart under him, slipping, becoming monstrous, always beyond reach. He cannot even think about the world let alone write or speak about it.

The second and more positive way in which Chandos describes his situation is to speak about a new revelation that seems to come to him miraculously at unpredictable moments and to be caused by seemingly indiscriminate sights or objects. He is at a loss to describe the feeling, writing, "There is something ineffable, you see, something one could probably never define, that makes itself known to me at such times, filling like a vessel some arbitrary feature of my everyday surroundings with a prodigal surge of more exalted life" (23). He lists some such objects or vessels as "A watering-can, a harrow left standing in a field, a dog in the sun, a rundown churchyard, a cripple, a small farmhouse" (23). As Chandos continues to expound on these moments of intensity, it becomes clear that they are providing him with a return to his former condition of oneness with the world. He writes,

> It strikes me then that everything, everything in this world, everything I can remember, everything that my most wayward thoughts might touch upon, is something after all...I have the feeling that my body is made up of nothing but ciphers, and that all things are therefore accessible to me...that we all might enter into a new communication with the whole of existence if we only began to think with our hearts. (27)

Chandos's new revelations and his old delirious feeling differ in two main ways. Firstly, where his previous sense of unity with the world was a constant presence in his life – informing his writing, his interaction with others, his movements, his senses – these new revelations are vexingly transitory and rare. Chandos finds himself actively searching "for that one object lying or leaning there unnoticed by anyone else, that one object whose unprepossessing form, whose simple, mute existence, can become the source of that puzzling, nameless, but unbounded delight" (29). In other words, formerly his life was full, composed of a vast interconnectedness between nature and culture, between objects and subjects; now, however, his life is an "almost unimaginable emptiness" (28) with the revelations as extraordinary points spacing out the ordinary blankness.

The other major difference between Chandos's previous and present ecstasies is that rather than compelling or *sourcing* his writing, his new experiences of the revelatory completely silence him: "Once the strange enchantment leaves me, I find I am left with nothing to say about it; I could no more relate in reasonable terms what it is that constitutes this harmony that weaves through me and the whole of the world…than I could detail the inner workings of my intestines or the coursing of my blood" (27-8). His chosen metaphor is interesting here, implying that should he have special knowledge or know a special language of his experience, he would be able to speak about it. Or, in fact, if he were *someone else*, a *doctor*, in this case, then the mysteries of the revelation would be clear to him. At the end of his letter, Chandos returns to this point in the passage which Coetzee has quoted for his Postscript: "The language in which it might have been given me to write, and even to do my thinking, is neither Latin nor English, nor Italian, nor Spanish, but one of which I know not a single word, one used by the dumbest of things in speaking with me, and one in which, perhaps, I will someday be called to account for myself from my grave before an unknown judge" (32). It is perhaps understood that the condition for this specialised language is death – surely death would close the paradox of a dumb language, an unknown judge, by bringing to life the words that synchronize with Chandos's revelation. Or, even more accurately, rather than pushing time forward to death, Chandos means to revert to a place prior to false and gratuitous language. Italo Calvino, a contemporary author whose books are also often preoccupied with the non-place before language writes in his 1968 story 'A Sign in Space':

> In my nostalgia, the first sign…remained beyond attacks of time and its changes, the sign created before the beginning of forms, which was to contain something that would have survived all forms, namely the fact of being a sign and nothing else. (1968: 37)

In this case, then, the specialised language belongs to those who have never known the present world, as it is now covered with "a general thickness of signs superimposed and coagulated…the universe scrawled over on all sides…There was no longer any way to establish a point of reference" (Calvino 1968: 39). For sentient humans, an impossible dimension.

*

Elizabeth felt she was going mad. Could it all be simply a coincidence? The Lord Chandos letter was dated, "This 22nd of August," the date of her own birthday. Coetzee's Lady Chandos letter was dated

"This 11 September," a date, of course, with spectacular significance since 2001, but with a particular significance to her the day she read it in 2003. The night before, after finishing the final Lesson of the book and deciding to leave the Postscript until morning, Elizabeth had had a dream. It was an apocalyptic terrifying dream from which she had woken breathless, crystal-clear images still playing in the centre of her memory. The images did not fade all day. The images were of New York City and herself at the top of a high rise building, caught in a tremendous cyclone.

And then she had read the *Postscript*. "This 11 September, AD 1603". A chill had run down her spine. It was the sixteenth of March that day.

She had shut the book quickly and gazed at the front cover: the Venus de Milo, framed with only the torso in view, rising from amongst the sea of a blurred modern crowd with one man's triple-imaged face looking upwards at the unseen head, his own expression caught in bewilderment and scorn.

Normally, when she told her dreams to her boyfriend, they were flat and boring; stupid, even to herself. This morning, he listened, captive. She surprised herself with the passion with which she told it. *I'll write it down*, she thought. But when she did, over a period of weeks, it lost its way. It thudded from her like a dropped sack.

*

Lady Chandos and the problem of metaphor

The Venus de Milo originally had arms, as everyone knows in the backs of their minds. One of Aphrodite's arms rested on a *herma*, or stone pillar, beside her, the other, it is debated, held an apple. However, the statue as it is now, standing in the Louvre museum in Paris, is, as it were, locked in stone in the collective imagination as an armless goddess. Although at the time of its finding in 1820 attempts were made to design new arms for the statue, King Louis XVIII later decreed that the natural beauty of the incomplete image should not be disturbed. In Coetzee's 2005 novel *Slow Man*, amputee Paul Rayment identifies in the statue a difference between art and humanity: "If it were discovered tomorrow that the Venus was in fact modelled on an amputee, she would be removed at once to a basement store. Why? Why can the fragmentary image of a woman be admired but not the image of a fragmentary woman?" (59). The double-affliction of the Venus mirrors the double-affliction of Lord Chandos, and in turn the coupled torment of Lord and Lady Chandos. Perhaps it is a stretch of analogy, but a connection could be made between this statue and Co-etzee's ideas about writing which he presents in his 'Postscript' and elsewhere in *Elizabeth Costello*; ideas which I argue in this book have actually carried through each of his novels so far. The written, sitting locked in its even black lines, gives the impression of belonging, of being primary; if one explores, however, into the region of its making, the situation, the hand, the pen of its origin, we might perhaps glimpse the shadow limbs, the amputated gestures that exist between the lines.

Coetzee's Lady Chandos letter, when read quickly, gives the impression of a desperate breathless back-and-forth motion, an anxi-ety and intense uneasiness. Again and again she begins to try and de-scribe her feelings about the situation she and her husband are in, and again and again she negates her attempted descriptions as *contagions*:

> Into me, soul and body, [my husband] presses what are no longer words but flaming swords. We are not meant to live thus, Sir. *Flaming swords* I say my Philip presses into me, swords that are not words; but they are neither flaming swords nor are they words. It is like a contagion, saying one thing always for another (*like a contagion*, I say)...*Always it is not what I say but some-thing else.* (Coetzee 2003a: 228)

On one level, it could be supposed that Hofmannsthal and Coetzee are attempting a clever irony in that although both Lord and Lady Chan-dos confess to a deep struggle with language, their respective letters are not only eloquent and finely-crafted, but stand solidly as statu-esque testament to their obvious ability to describe and express. It is the kind of comedy or writerly half-lie that Maurice Blanchot speaks of at the beginning of 'From Dread to Language': "[The writer] speaks the language of men at the moment when there is no longer, for him, either language or man" (1999: 343). This irony, however, is self-aware, and whatever cleverness or humour such an oxymoronic joke could contain is overridden by the serious distress of the couple's pleas to Bacon. "Save me, dear Sir, save my husband! Write!" Lady Chandos writes, and later, "Drowning, we write out of our separate fates. Save us" (Coetzee 2003a: 229-230). Lady Chandos is not only asking for salvation from the first aspect of their affliction, the fragmenting of language, "where words give way beneath your feet like rotting boards (*like rotting boards* I say again, I cannot help myself...)" (228). She is also asking for salvation from the second, from the revelatory: "*We are not made for revelation*, I want to cry out, *nor I nor you, my Philip*, revelation that sears the eye like staring into the sun" (229). It is only for "extreme souls" to live thus, she writes, and only in a time "when giants or perhaps angels stride the earth" (228-9).

What Lord and Lady Chandos are describing, it seems, are the two extremes of the same unbearable silence. On the one hand, language is 'decaying' and 'rotting' on their tongues and beneath their feet when they try to speak of everyday concepts. On the other hand they are experiencing "*presences of the infinite*" (Coetzee 2003a: 230), extraordinary and rare moments for which there is no language available at all. In his essay 'Literature and the Right to Death,' Blanchot speaks of two similar extremes, describing them as *slopes*. The first is meaningful prose, its goal being to "express things in a language that designates things according to what they mean" (Blanchot 1995: 332). This process, however, brings about a negation where the "indeterminate" is "destroyed in order to be known, subjugated, communicated" (338, 330). The realisation of this negation, it seems, is what Lord Chandos is battling with when he can no longer speak normally to his daughter. The second slope that Blanchot describes is concerned with "what things and beings would be if there were no world," (333) or as Michael Marais puts it in an essay on Coetzee and Blanchot, "things prior to their negation by language and human systems of order" (2000: 161). The Chandoses' experiences of ineffable revelation seem to apply to this category or slope. There they are in the valley between the slopes: as Marais goes on to write: "Literature's treacherous ambiguity derives from the fact that in writing, the writer is caught and suspended between day and night, between two slopes which are both necessary and impossible" (162).[2]

It is significant that the Chandoses are writing to Sir Francis Bacon, Lord Verulam and Viscount of St. Albans, the famous philosopher, statesman and a leading thinker in the new scientific method of analogous induction or 'ampliative inference'. Where previously

---

[2] Marais paraphrases here from Simon Critchley's 1997 *Very Little...Almost Nothing: Death, Philosophy, Literature.* New York: Routledge: 62-63.

scientists and logicians practised induction by drawing general conclusions from a particular instance, Francis Bacon's method was to
infer by way of analogy, working from similarities within the larger
group back to the particular and correcting errors according to experience later. Scientific hypotheses and the advancement of empiricism
were greatly improved by Bacon's contribution.

An analogy, as opposed to a metaphor or simile, is not,
strictly, a figure of speech. It is something observed rather than interpreted, a direct relation or similarity between two entities rather than a
forged link: *the analogy between the heart and a pump*. Where 'scientific' analogies such as this seek to make clear an otherwise obscure,
even miraculous, bodily role, metaphors and similes seek to problema-
tise and subvert, to make poetic as it were, the unmiraculous or taken-
for-granted. Jacques Lacan insisted on this distinction in his exposi-
tion of pathological symptoms as being structured like a language:
"Analogy is not metaphor...it was by deliberately avoiding analogy
that Freud opened up the right way to the interpretation of dreams, and
so to the notion of analytic symbolism" (Lacan 1977: 53). What Lord
and Lady Chandos are battling with is a sense that everything is either
an analogy or metaphor-simile. That there is nothing that is not a reference point for something else – whether the language-expression is
seeking to clarify or subvert. Lady Chandos is thwarted at every turn,
both when she tries to analogise her raptures (as flaming swords,
plagues of rats, contagions), and when she attempts to make a metaphor of the ordinary: "A dog sitting in a patch of sun licking itself...is
at one moment a dog and at the next a vessel of revelation" (Coetzee
2003a: 229).

This is a problem, perhaps *the* problem, entrenched within every act of
writing, whether subconscious or self-conscious. What the Chandoses
are experiencing, in a desperate physical way, is a central intersection
for literary theory that has been felt in different ways during recent
periods of literary endeavour: romanticism, realism, Russian formal-
ism, modernism, structuralism, poststructuralism. It is the problem of
the relationship between language and the world, also an ancient problem, encapsulated in Lady Chandos's cry of "*Always it is not what I
say but something else!*" And this 'something else' has been named
and re-named and finally unnamed by the same literary theorists: God,
the ineffable, being, the Other, space, silence. Lord and Lady Chan-

dos's aphasic disturbances seem to be concerned with something always overriding linguistic structure. Their struggle with language is not so much a question of *how exactly* language is scrambling in their minds, whether it is some impairment, more or less severe, of the faculty either for selection and substitution or for combination and contexture, as Roman Jakobson writes in his essay on the dual nature of language and aphasia (1987: 95-100). Rather, their struggle addresses the questions: *why* is this happening; *whether* it can ever not happen.

If metaphor is, as Lady Chandos, baulking, suggests, a state of being, a world – "All is allegory, says my Philip. Each creature is key to all other creatures" (Coetzee 2003a: 229) – then could it be possible for this tortured couple to ever delight in this world, to be sustained by it? Charles Simic, a poet whose metaphors strive to trap the being of an object, and who is influenced by surrealist philosophy, seeks out a space "below language...that place of original action and desire...a world where magic is possible, where chance reigns, where metaphors have their supreme logic" (Simic in Stocks 1991: 901). Is this the same world that Lady Chandos describes using the terrifying images of giants and angels striding the earth, "A time when such *extreme souls* as I write of may be able to bear their affliction" (Coetzee 2003a: 229). Where Simic and others like fellow poet Vasko Popa and Russian theorist Victor Shklovsky see the defamiliarising nature of metaphor and its all-encompassing quality, as something necessary, even beautiful, the Chandoses are horrified at its prospect. They want, and fear, as perhaps people everywhere simultaneously want and fear, a communication with no incalculable gaps between speaker, listener and said; with no innumerable instances of mishearing, misinterpretation, slippage, rupture, displacement. They long with the yen of the falling and dying for this *other language*, for the language of objects, the language of embodiment, the language in which they can call themselves to account.

The Lady Chandos letter comes with all the characteristics of a skilful surprising Postscript – it offers a sudden, even jarring, otherness that speaks from a distance to the story, ideas and lessons in the preceding narration. The character, Elizabeth Chandos, is an obscure, but trackable one with a neat trick to her name that gives her an affinity (perhaps she is an historical mirror-image) with the main character Elizabeth Costello. The sentences on the page, though stylistically familiar, are imbued with a sense of exteriority: this is, after all, an

addendum, an afterthought. The themes and images also ring bells –
animals, metaphor, visions – but come together here in a strange impassioned way in a voice we do not recognise as Costello's. What
does a Postscript like this do to the reader? In this case it presents an
opportunity for another reading of the text, a rethinking of its themes,
character and centre. Also, in its distance, the Postscript allows for
reflection on not only the writer Costello or the writer Lord Chandos,
but on the writer Coetzee who, in paralleling himself with Hofmannsthal, has revealed himself a little. Surely these are the quanda-
ries, like quarries, which the writer treads precariously between whenever he sets pen to paper: why do I write? what good does it do? is
there anything outside metaphor? doesn't that dog sitting in the sun
tell more than a million pages in a million books? Does *Elizabeth
Costello*, a story about an ageing writer reconsidering her life's work,
also tell the story of a dying age reconsidering the place, purpose and
value of its art?

The Author Divided in Coetzee's Novels

One step away from the blank page is the marked page.

The pen rests on the page and leaves a mark: instantly everything is different. The page has moved from being a negative, a 'what is not,' the despondent muteness of the Chandoses, into being divided: pen-mark and white space. It is now both at once. What is the relationship between the two: does one encroach upon, even usurp the other? Do they rest upon each other like two leaning playing cards? Are they warring? Do they make love? The marked page is caught up in, or perhaps is the inscription of, the divided author and the divided reader. It is the end-point of a slow descent, fraught with questions and doubts, the first indication that within the author the decision to write co-exists with the blankness of the decision to not write.

The divided author, and the split comes at the instant of the mark, is one reason the moment of putting pen to paper is excruciating. It is also another of J. M. Coetzee's enduring preoccupations which in *Elizabeth Costello* is unleashed, roaming through the Lessons, presenting a different face in each. One of the first impressions we have of Elizabeth Costello, the author, is that she is not whole, or in one piece. Her division tells us not only about herself as a writer, but about Coetzee the divided author who also creates (must create?) divided characters. Is she a person, for instance, or a vehicle, set on the tracks, for enunciating ideas? In a demonstration of Coetzee's own double-sidedness, an interjection in Lesson 1 tells us what is being enacted: "Realism has never been comfortable with ideas…So when it needs to debate ideas, as here, realism is driven to invent situations – walks in the countryside, conversations – in which characters give voice to contending ideas and thereby in a certain sense embody them" (Coetzee 2003a: 9). This is only one of the divides present in the book, both embodied by Elizabeth Costello herself and reproduced critically by Coetzee.

This chapter will examine some of the other significant divides or doubles present in Coetzee's work including: the author as both continuing in time and existing in time's rupture; the author as both particular person and common passageway – thus the author as both enacting a performance of literature, and catching glimpses of the Law of literature, and thus the author as both human and divine. Aside from these internal divides, there is the crucial divide that separates Elizabeth Costello from J. M. Coetzee, that between an author and their character – to what extent is this, in fact, another internal divide?

The significance of these divides for the question of the moment of writing and the value of literature will be discussed with reference to a number of Coetzee's works. It is this book's contention, in fact, that the two latest books *Elizabeth Costello* and *Slow Man* call for a rereading of Coetzee's previous works. These books refer to, adjust, reassess and in fact rewrite those works which are considered synonymous with Coetzee's style and voice: *Life and Times of Michael K, Waiting for the Barbarians, Foe, Disgrace*, and so on. The refocusing upon the role of author, and the direction towards autobiography raises questions regarding subjectivity and ageing, as will be discussed here with reference to Said's posthumous 'Thoughts on Late Style.'

That slow moment when pen hits page resounds through Coetzee's works, unavoidably, and endlessly. One is led to the place where the book was conceived, to the ink, the nib, the pen, and necessarily to the hand around the pen, the mind that asks the hand to move here and there about the page. The nature of the author, as figured by Coetzee, is always one of division, the separation of a wall or window, it being held there by the tension of the divide.

A Moment of Rupture: The white-haired woman

We speak of the dog with the sore foot *or* the bird with the broken wing. *But the dog does not think of itself in those terms, or the bird. To the dog, when it tries to walk, there is simply* I am pain, *to the bird, when it launches itself into flight, simply* I cannot. *With us it seems to be different… The existence of such common locutions [as 'my leg,' 'my body'] shows that language cannot get purchase, cannot get going, until it has split up the unity of experience.*
- J. M. Coetzee, *Diary of a Bad Year*

There is one section of *Elizabeth Costello* that stands out apart from the others, striking the pose, in its language of myth, of a key that will unlock the mysteries of all that has preceded it. In Lesson 8 we find the dreamlike postlude, the death in fact, that patterns a number of Coetzee's other works. *Age of Iron* ends with a scene of abstraction, Mrs Curren asking 'Is it time?' before being embraced "with mighty force, so that the breath went out of me in a rush," by the silent death-herald Vercueil (Coetzee 1990: 198). *Foe* also finishes with the surreal final exhalation of the drowned Friday, "From inside him comes a slow stream, without breath, without interruption" (Coetzee 1986a: 157). Death also comes in abstraction here in Lesson 8, with the parable of Costello's calling. It seems an appropriate beginning to a chapter on the two sides of the author, as figuring prominently in Lesson 8 is a Wall.

Lesson 8 'At the Gate,' as Elizabeth Costello herself points out, bears striking resemblances in both scenery and tone, to Kafka's story 'Before the Law' which appears as a short story in its own right and within his novel *The Trial*: "The wall, the gate, the sentry, are straight out of Kafka. So is the demand for a confession, so is the courtroom…Kafka, but only the superficies of Kafka, Kafka reduced and flattened to a parody" (Coetzee 2003a: 209). In fact, she finds herself in a falsely literary place – the panel of judges are *"Excessively literary…A caricaturist's idea of a bench of judges"* (200). Later during another interrogation, Costello is asked about the voices that summon her to write and is reminded of Joan of Arc's interrogation: *"How do you know where your voices come from?* She cannot stand the literariness of it all. Have they not the wit to come up with something new?" (204). The writer has found herself in "someone's idea of what hell would be like for a writer, or at least a purgatory: a purgatory of clichés" (206). The town itself, the state of limbo, signifies this between-ness, the gate being the midpoint. The surreal image of purgatory is one that has repeated through Coetzee's books, from *In the Heart of the Country* and Magda's mid-existence in the veld: "What purgatory to live in this insentient universe where everything but me is merely itself!" (Coetzee 1977: 73) to *Age of Iron* in which Mrs Curren, dying of cancer, is at one point admitted to hospital: "Don't you know the rule? This is the house of shadow and suffering through which you must pass on the way to death. That is the sentence passed upon all: a term in prison before the execution" (Coetzee 1990: 69-70).

Elizabeth Costello's final look at the gate, the near final words of the book itself, concern a vision she has of a dog lying at the foot of the gate: "It is her first vision in a long while, and she does not trust it, does not trust in particular the anagram GOD-DOG. *Too literary*, she thinks again. A curse on literature!" (Coetzee 2003a: 224-225). She has found herself, presumably at the end of her life, in a place of weak puns and obvious allegories, of cute references and cheesy intertextuality: she has found herself, it seems, in a badly written book. Interestingly enough, though in all probability an unintended coincidence for Coetzee, the final words spoken by K in Kafka's *The Trial* are 'Like a dog!' (Kafka 1994: 178). The expression has echoed before in Coetzee's *Disgrace*, a book 'peopled' with dogs. The last words of chapter 22 are Lucy's as she resigns herself to giving up her property, her home, her dignity to her neighbour Petrus, "Yes, like a dog" (Coetzee 1999a: 205). In *Slow Man*, Paul Rayment's notion that he might be "on the other side" comes about because of a single word: "Quite a leap to make, from the word *D-O-G* in a notebook to life after death" (Coetzee 2005: 123). The pun which exasperates Costello so much has its own kind of history, another inkling of an important divide: the animal, the divine. In this world, then, Lady Chandos's cry, *"Always it is not what I say but something else,"* which the reader will come across very shortly, has an exasperatingly literal meaning for the author Costello. For she knows better than anyone the kinds of tricks a well-placed reference may play in the meaning of a book.

The climactic point of Kafka's 'Before the Law' is the final line in which the countryman is told by the gatekeeper, "No one else could ever be admitted here, since this gate was made only for you. I am now going to shut it" (Kafka 1958: 129). Costello also guesses that the gate before which she supplicates is *her* gate: "Evidently her gate, and hers alone, though it must be visible to anyone who cares to give it a glance" (Coetzee 2003a: 223). The question she asks herself is why has *she*, specifically she, been given this false, literary, Kafkaesque, intensely clichéd place in which to spend her final days? Costello doesn't even like Kafka, she finds him, or at least his K selves, "simply childish" (209). The answer to this question seems not to be, in the end, a series of connections or locations between Costello and her new circumstances – her life and now her judgement – but rather a series of dislocations between her various versions of self, belief and autonomy.

The opening paragraph of Lesson 8 gives a clue to this new rendering of Costello's fractured identity:

> It is a hot afternoon. The square is packed with visitors. Few spare a glance for the white-haired woman who, suitcase in hand, descends from the bus. She wears a blue cotton frock; her neck, in the sun, is burned red and beaded with sweat. (193)

The style and perspective of this opening section is unique to the book. In most chapters, Elizabeth Costello is simply reintroduced as 'She' in the opening lines. In Lessons 3 and 4, the perspective shifts slightly as Costello is introduced as her son's mother. In Lesson 1, 'Realism', after an overture to the book itself, Costello is introduced with a sharp parody of realism: "Elizabeth Costello is a writer, born in 1928, which makes her sixty-six years old, going on sixty-seven..." (1). With each new succeeding 'She' Elizabeth Costello is relaunched as this same sixty-six year old writer with nine novels, two children and two marriages behind her (although of these last not another word is spoken). In the chapters involving her son and her son's family, Costello is seen from a slightly different angle, as mother, mother-in-law and grandmother, and her identity is expanded accordingly. In Lesson 8, however, Elizabeth Costello is "the white-haired woman" in the blue cotton frock, sunburnt and sweating. The image reminds the reader of another more personal instance, back in Lesson 1; an impression Elizabeth's son John has when they arrive at their hotel after a long journey: "She is still wearing the old blue raincoat she wore from the airport. Her hair has a greasy, lifeless look" (3). What does this 'second look,' this stranger-making mean in terms of Elizabeth Costello's identity as a writer; how does the 'literariness' of her limbo, and its literary repercussions, retell the moment of writing and readdress the value of literature?

Time, tense, and aspect

In his essay 'Time, Tense, and Aspect in Kafka's "The Burrow,"' Coetzee discusses the "relations between the *time of narration* (the moving *now* of the narrator's utterance) and the *time of the narrative* (referential time)" (Coetzee 1981: 557). He is particularly interested in the rhetoric of iteration within the narrative and the way in which time is somehow collapsed for the burrowing creature: "The inability to learn from past failure is a reflection of the fact that the iterations are not ordered: none of them being earlier in time than any other, no iteration encompasses a memory of an earlier one" (564). Coetzee contrasts two kinds of awareness of time and uses this contrast to conclude that the collapse of narrative time equals the responsibility of the time of narration:

> The first, which we can call historical awareness, imputes reality to a past that it sees as continuous with the present The second, which we can call eschatological, recognizes no such continuity: there is only the present, which is always present, separated from Ingarden's 'dead past' by a moment of rupture…Now that the construct of narrative time has collapsed, there is only the time of narration left, the shifting *now* within which his narrative takes place, leaving behind it a wake (a text). (578)

In his famous essay 'The Novel Today,' Coetzee again addresses the question of history, this time focussing on the novel rather than narrative:

> In times of intense ideological pressure like the present, when the space in which the novel and history normally coexist like two cows on the same pasture, each minding its own business, is squeezed almost to nothing, the novel, it seems to me, has only two options: supplementarity or rivalry…[storytelling is] more venerable than history, as ancient as the cockroach. (Coetzee 1988b: 3-4)

Lesson 8 is not only Kafkaesque in the various paraphernalia of court-room and allegorical gate, but in its narrative relation and its moment of rupture. It is a text to which narrative time and history, in terms of memory and change, is insignificant or is referred to, in Coetzee's metaphor, as part of the wake left behind by the time of narration: "Even in this town time passes. The day arrives, her day" (Coetzee 2003a: 198). In contrast to the preceding chapters in which Costello moves fairly realistically through consecutive times and locations, here time is pointedly a necessity of the narration, a way for the story to continue, literally a way for the blank page to be filled, Costello's blank page and Coetzee's: "With his left hand he pushes a sheet of paper across to her. She lets go of her suitcase and picks up the paper. It is blank. 'Before I pass through I must make a statement,' she repeats" (194). As discussed earlier, Coetzee is interested in the middle voice of a text, defining this voice as *having reference to the self* (Coetzee 1984b: 11). Here we perhaps find an example of the text's own middle voice: a moment of rupture whereby the continuation of the narrative, the furtherance of Elizabeth Costello herself, is dependent solely, and consciously, on its continuing to be written.

Anne Waldron Neumann wrote an article in 1990 on present-tense narration in Coetzee's 1980 novel *Waiting for the Barbarians*, one of her enquiries being: "How does the present-tense narration complicate our task of imagining a fictional occasion of the story's narrating?"(Neumann 1990: 65). The question could be asked of almost all Coetzee's works, his present-tense narration being one the most distinctive elements of his writing-style. Neumann cites Dorrit Cohn proposing in 1989 that stories written in "this synchronic manner" could be on the way to "establishing a new literary convention," one as "unnatural" as the third-person omniscient (66).[3] Neumann's insightful conclusion is that Coetzee, who was later the subject of condemnation for his apparent evasion of political responsibility, has presented, "in a situation of such extreme political and economic oppression as South Africa's – where even visions, if they are too specific, can seem to impose a history – an unspecified, ahistorical allegory [which] may make a more acceptable offering" (Neumann 1990: 81). The response is a perfectly sound one for a book such as *Barbarians*, but what of less extremely political books, written during less extreme times?

A survey of Coetzee's works tells us that of his twelve books of fiction (including *Youth, Boyhood* and *Slow Man*) only two of them (*Dusklands* and *Foe*) include a substantial past-tense subdivision and only one of them (*Michael K*) begins and ends in the past tense (though the middle section II, from the perspective of the doctor, is written in the first person present). Neumann hints at a broader explanation for the tense-perspective when she makes comparisons between the Magistrate and Coetzee as an allegory of authorship, but she continues to shy away from this most personal assumption with hesitant phrases like, "suggesting a shame Coetzee may feel about partly earn-

---

[3] Neumann is here citing Cohn, D. 1989. 'Fictional *versus* Historical Lives: Borderlines and Borderline Cases' in *The Journal of Narrative Technique* 19: 19.

ing *his* keep from allegories of South African political agony" (Neumann 1990: 76). Surely, however, a stronger association between the author's writing and the character's soliloquy presents the most interesting solution to the problem of fictional occasion. In fact it is very often the case in Coetzee's present-tense works that since a realistic or referential time of narrative is "ruled out," as Neumann puts it, it is the moving 'now' that becomes the reader's principal entry.

Coetzee's work is rarely considered an example of postmodern play. As Derek Attridge writes in his book *J. M. Coetzee and the Ethics of Reading*: "To locate Coetzee in the tradition of postmodern playfulness, teasing the reader with fictional truths and truthful fictions, is to overlook the much more important engagement in his work with the demands and responsibilities of writing and reading" (Attridge 2004: 199). Without making a judgement about the relative 'importance' of these writers' engagements, one can still find, as through my brief analysis of tense in Coetzee's novels, a residing, almost inevitable, reference to the self (or reference to the writer) in any one of Coetzee's works. The moving *now*, which the reader must accept since a realistic fictional occasion collapses, is (or was once) the moving *now* for the writer, for the pen. It is my argument that one cannot read Coetzee's novels without being made aware of the creation of the text, the unmistakeable movement of pen across page: the excruciating moment is present for the reader in the shifting *now* of narration. Here self-reflexivity, an old technique with which postmodernists have played many delightful, if sometimes crude, tricks, is at its most subtle and embodied.

Nowhere is this more in evidence than in *Elizabeth Costello*, with a character whose appendage, 'the novelist', follows her around like 'the Great' or 'the Conqueror'. Although the third-person narration is a remove from the first-person of *Barbarians*, the closeness of this third person (as though scurrying around with pen and paper, transposing her lectures word-for-word, watching her sigh and collapse into bed at night) creates a distinctive connection between author and author-character. Who else could follow her as "Head down, meeting no one's eye, she pushes her way to the ladies' room and shuts herself in a cubicle" (Coetzee 2003a: 176). Coetzee, the surreptitious third person, has himself read out the words of Costello's lectures to crowds at conferences and festivals, and it is easy to imagine him weaving in and out of Costello's life and person. This connection will be further discussed in the section dealing with authors and characters. Here suffice to say that when, in Lesson 6, Costello attempts to rewrite her paper, striking out paragraphs and pages, scribbling revisions in the margins, until she "stares in dismay at the mess" (Coetzee 2003a: 164), the reader inevitably allows their eye to trace the straight, neat margins and wonder what kind of muddle *this* book was once in – and, perhaps, still is.

Time, in the book, is cut up, often pointedly, into manageable chunks as Costello zips, in the turning of a page, from Melbourne, to Amsterdam, to Pennsylvania, to rural Zululand. The moment of rupture is signified in Lesson 8 by Costello's reintroduction as 'the white-haired woman'. No longer is Costello travelling to fixed destinations which have their probable counterparts in the real world, no longer is she relentlessly pursued by her twenty-word biography: " 'Elizabeth Costello, noted Australian novelist and essayist, author of *The House on Eccles Street* and many other books'…Frozen in the past, as usual; frozen in the achievements of her youth" (161). Instead she is dislocated and reduced, *one of many* attempting to summarise their belief. At the end of her story, the gatekeeper says finally, "All the time…We see people like you all the time" (225). What Costello seems to be encountering is the paradox between herself as a distinctive being – an old woman in an inappropriate dress with her own name ("her name is not fading away, not in the least" (214)), and body, "this gentle lumbering monster that has been given to her to look after" (210), with her own gate and her own purgatory. A paradox between this woman and herself as writer, storyteller, "secretary of the invisible" (199) (a phrase she has borrowed from Czeslaw Milosz), hearer, visionary – a mythological passageway, devoid of specificity. In this place, it is all that is considered meaningful, since her history, her passage through time, has been eliminated, poised as she is on the edge of infinity. The question arises: what is a writer without time; without the passage of pen across page? What is a writer without her books?

Singing birds

At her first appearance in court in Lesson 8, Costello opens her revised statement with the words:

> I am a writer. You may think I should say instead, I was a writer.
> But I am or was a writer because of who I am or was. I have not

> ceased to be what I am. As yet. Or so it feels to me. (Coetzee 2003a: 199)

At her second hearing, when asked if she has altered the basis of her plea between hearings, Costello responds:

> You ask if I have changed my plea. But who am I, who is this *I* this *you*. We change from day to day, and we also stay the same. No *I*, no *you* is more fundamental than any other. You might as well ask which is the true Elizabeth Costello: the one who made the first statement or the one who made the second. My answer is, both are true. Both. And neither. *I am an other.* (221)

At this, her panel "cannot contain themselves," they "abandon all dignity and howl with laughter" (221).

Her first hearing, in effect, in which she argues that, as a writer, "It is not my profession to believe, just to write" (194), can be seen now, in light of this second hearing, as a circular argument, a tautology. Costello seems to be saying that *when she is her writer self*, then she can have no beliefs – beliefs can only pass through her from elsewhere, she can only perform, or take dictation, or act as medium. It is when she is a writer that her beliefs dissolve: it is only when she has no beliefs that she is able to write. At her second hearing, on the other hand, Costello tells a story that some reviewers have mythologised into being the ultimate conclusion to *Elizabeth Costello*'s running argument between embodiment and reason. Her story is a memory from her childhood about the frogs of the river Dulgannon who hibernate during the dry season and become like the dead, buried in coffins of mud, until the rain awakes them and again they fill the river with their "chorus of joyous belling" (217). The story is beautifully told, the frogs linger in the imagination, their weblike fingers and their cycle of death and resurrection. At the end, however, Costello says, "Excuse my language…Usually I take care to conceal the extravagances of the imagination. But today, for this occasion, I thought I would conceal nothing, bare all" (216-7).

Elizabeth Costello does not tell them that she has used the technique of passion on advice from the cleaning woman "who put her up to it" (218). She does not tell them that when she applies her writer's test to the story of the frogs later, it gives off "no tone at all" (219). She conceals her inclination to pronounce as vapid the judge's conclusion that she believes in life. She is silent when asked directly whether she grew up on the Dulgannon at all. One can only assume, as the judges do, that when Costello says "Today I stand before you not as a writer but as an old woman who was once a child, telling you what I remember of the Dulgannon mudflats" (217) she is telling a lie. Or rather, she is putting on a performance, something she has done her whole life.

At one point in Coetzee's 1990 novel *Age of Iron*, the narrator, Mrs Curren[4], has a remarkable dream. She sees her housekeeper Florence with her two children Hope and Beauty, all three of them masked, walking like goddesses through a festive crowd. Mrs Curren herself is "to provide a show" (Coetzee 1990: 177). She stands in the street, opposite the Parliament buildings "circled by people, doing my tricks with fire…Burning, doing my show, I stand transfixed". When she awakes, Mrs Curren recognises the vision as being from outside time:

> Forever the goddess is passing, forever, caught in a posture of surprise and regret, I do not follow. Though I peer and peer into the vortex from which visions come, the wake of the goddess and her god-children remains empty, the woman who should follow behind not there, the woman with serpents of flame in her hair who beats her arms and cries and dances. (178)

More than anything (more perhaps than being a vision of politics, race, war, justice or guilt) it seems this is a vision of the writer. The writer performing, dancing, enveloped in agonizing flames and forever peering into the vortex, the wake, from which visions come – barred from this vortex. The writer, enthralled with the performance, never stepping from the stage and into the source. And, most strikingly, the writer excluded from the normal passage of time, "transfixed".

Elizabeth Costello, too, is charged with being a performer. In Lesson 8, the woman with the Polish accent from her dormitory, whom Costello thinks of as the Kapo, instructs her in the ways of the examinations: "It is not belief that the boards are after. The effect is enough, the effect of belief…We call ourselves the singing-birds. We

---

[4] In later interviews Coetzee speaks of his protagonist as 'Elizabeth Curren' (see Coetzee 1992: 250, 340), however in the novel only her initials E. C. and surname are revealed.

sing for the boards, for their delight" (Coetzee 2003a: 214). Earlier in
the book her son compares her to a circus seal: "One more time she
must heave herself up on to the tub, one more time show that she can
balance the ball on her nose" (3). And later, she herself, with reference
to the collapse of realism, admits: "There used to be a time, we believe, when we could say who we were. Now we are just performers
speaking our parts" (19). Here again is Costello's paradox between the
singular and the essential, between the rupture of time and the continuation of time. Her picture of belief is of a girl crossing a stream,
"pausing balancing, then moving on" (222), but does *Belief*, like *Law*,
demand something essential, something outside of the self – a still full
pool, not a skipping, dipping chase?

Derek Attridge, in his Epilogue on *Elizabeth Costello* from *J.
M. Coetzee and the Ethics of Reading* cites Costello's frog story and
her stepping-stone image of belief in arguing that "what has mattered,
for Elizabeth Costello and for the reader, is the event…of storytelling,
of testing, of self-questioning, and not the outcome" (Attridge 2004:
205). It is certainly true that Coetzee withholds any tidy conclusions to
any of the Costello episodes. It could be said that one of the most consistent themes of *Elizabeth Costello* is uncertainty or inconsistency.
Immediately after giving each of her celebrity-lectures Costello is,
without fail, challenged by someone in attendance; she responds, usually feebly, and in some cases ends up mortified and doubtful of her
own premise, as in this exchange from 'The Lives of Animals':

> 'But your own vegetarianism, Mrs Costello…it comes out of
> moral conviction, does it not?'
> 'No, I don't think so,' says his mother. 'It comes out of a desire to
> save my soul.' […]
> 'Well, I have a great respect for it,' says Garrard. 'As a way of
> life.'
> 'I'm wearing leather shoes,' says his mother. 'I'm carrying a
> leather purse. I wouldn't have overmuch respect if I were you.'
> (Coetzee 2003a: 89)

Rather than being an observation or even celebration of the uncertain
literary event, I would argue that the sadness and desperation so evident in the *Elizabeth Costello* Postscript is also echoed, less plainly,
throughout the book. It is the same sadness: arising from a profound
realisation of the paradox between literature the event and literature
the law.

Taking Kafka's story 'Before the Law' as his primary text (as does Coetzee's Lesson 8), Jacques Derrida's essay of the same name discusses the collision between the singular text and literary essence, or 'the name of the law': "There is a singularity about relationship to the law, a law of singularity which must come into contact with the general or universal essence of the law without ever being able to do so" (Derrida 1992: 187). He goes on to write specifically about the Kafka story: "This text, this singular text…names and relates in its way this conflict without encounter between law and singularity, this *paradox* or *enigma* of being-before-the-law" (187). What Costello's uncertainty speaks to, what the uncomfortable jolt of an articulate protagonist's ambiguity, even disgrace, addresses is Derrida's and Kafka's paradox between law and singularity. When Elizabeth Costello writes on her blank page words which are uncertain, susceptible to change, words which could very well be other words, and then reads them to a body of academics, or students, passengers on a cruise ship, or a panel of judges, the "conflict without encounter" between firmness, timelessness or law and fickleness, shiftiness or singularity registers as a paradox. It seems Costello is *partaking* of the law, using it, presenting it, singing it, providing an illusion of it, while never being able to reach it. So while, as Derrida states "there is no such thing as a literary essence" (187) or *law*, since it is intolerant of its own history, still its presence is somehow necessary *as* the unreachable – the guarded gate, the forbidden light, the goal.

As Richard Beardsworth observes, Derrida, in refuting Freud's attempt to relate the event of the origin of moral law, and in deconstructing Freud's story of the original crime, discovers the ability of literature to both express and embody the *différance* of the law. This *différance* being explained as such: "If the law is, on the one hand, unaccountable, on the other hand it is *nowhere* but *in* its inscriptions in history, whilst not being reducible *to* these inscriptions either" (Beardsworth 1996: 29). Derrida uses the term *fictive narrativity* which he describes as "fiction *of* narration as well as fiction as narration: fictive narration as the simulacrum of narration and not only as the narration of an imaginary history" (Derrida 1992: 199). Thus Freud's account of the origin of the law in 'Totem and Taboo' is "the origin of literature at the same time as the origin of law…a story told, a spreading rumour, without author or end" (Derrida 1992: 199). So much modern literature, as Beardsworth comments, contains the mark

of fictive narrativity, literature which "remarks its 'literariness'"
(1996: 37). Whether it is Flaubert calling speech a "cracked cauldron
on which we knock out tunes for dancing-bears" (Flaubert 1992: 154),
or Italo Svevo's character Emilio finding "he could no longer think
with a pen in his hand" (Svevo 1993: 184); whether it is Durrell's
Pursewarden frustrated with writers returning to the question of literature "like a tongue to a hollow tooth" (Durrell 1960: 125), or Carey's
Jack Maggs discovering that to the eminent writer Tobias Oates he is
merely a character in a novel (Carey 1997: 353-4). And thus with
Kafka's 'Before the Law' where the "non-origin of the origin of the
law is reinscribed as both the *content* of Kafka's tale – the deferment
of the man of the country's access to the Law – and...the very *'event'*
of the text" (Beardsworth 1996: 35) (my emphasis). Beardsworth implies here that the event of the text also embodies a deferment, that
literature *is* deferment, the embodiment of *différance*.

     To defer: perhaps another of Coetzee's middle voice verbs,
neither passive nor active. In her state of unfinished limbo, Costello
does not revel in, as perhaps a genuinely postmodern author would, as
Schelling put it, "an eternal round of propositions, each dissolving into
its opposite, a chaos in which no element can crystallize" (Schelling
1980: 84). She is rather "in a dark mood," (Coetzee 2003a: 222) repelled by food, sleep and sun, and finally as desperate, as "out of control" (224) as Lady Chandos.

     In dialogue with Claire Parnet, Gilles Deleuze discusses the
superiority of Anglo-American literature. He says that literature and
its characters should be formed as a line of flight, literally in Melville's case, a flight to the ocean and a new horizon: "In them everything is departure, becoming, passage, leap, daemon, relationship with
the outside" (Deleuze and Parnet 2002: 36). Citing structuralism as a
system of "points and positions," Deleuze criticises the French for
their "search for a primary certainty as a point of origin, always a
point of anchor" (37, 39). It is the middle which is interesting, he says,
not the fixed points of beginning or end. To illustrate this line of flight
between two points, Deleuze speaks of a double betrayal – two faces
turning away from each other: "It is in this double turning-away, in
the divergence of faces, that the line of flight – that is, the deterritori-
alization of man – is traced" (40).

     In the case of Kafka's 'Before the Law' and Coetzee's 'At the
Gate,' the two figures of supplicant and gatekeeper are not turning

away from, but towards each other, still facing different directions. It is a picture that reminds one, again, of the double-image of the writer. To cite Blanchot's memorable illustration once more:

> The existence of the writer is proof that within one individual there exist side by side both a man full of dread and one who is cool and calculating, both a madman and a reasonable being, a mute who has lost all words firmly wedded to an orator, master of discourse. The case of the writer is special because he represents the paradox of dread in a special way. Dread challenges all the realities of reason, its methods, its possibilities, its very capacity to exist, its ends, and yet dread forces reason to be there. (Blanchot 1999: 346)

A writer could write endlessly. Costello's choice of song, as she calls it, about the Dulgannon frogs is meaningful only for the fact that it is randomly chosen and performed from the infinite fictions she could have told. Facing down this endlessness, however, staring at the face of the possibility of everything, is the possibility of nothing. And in the writer, the two possibilities face each other. It is here that Derrida's, Deleuze's and Blanchot's images converge. At some point meaning is unaccountable, but on the other hand, it is endlessly accountable. As the writer puts pen to paper there occurs a consciousness of a divide between the individual and the archetype. Mirroring this divide is Derrida's conflict without encounter between literature the Law and literature the act. Here too is Blanchot's mute and orator and Deleuze's double betrayal. In a short story called 'Borges and Myself,' Jorge Luis Borges divides himself the 'I' from Borges the writer. He writes: "I live, I let myself live, so that Borges can weave his tales and poems, and those tales and poems are my justification" (Borges 1970: 151). Here is a story that would clearly not exist without a consciousness of the author divided, and it is my contention that neither would the book *Elizabeth Costello*, nor Kafka's 'Before the Law,' nor perhaps any text that follows the line of flight. The story itself will divulge its moment of conception. It is between the points, the girl in mid-leap from one stepping-stone to the next, that belief exists and stories are told. Whether this is self-fulfilling, whether this between-ness or both-ness could be considered satisfactory to a text without outcome, is another matter altogether.

*

She has brown hair and a name, *Elizabeth*. What does her blue dress look like? She once owned one, when she was fourteen. A hideous thing, but back then she thought it wistful. She bought it from *black rose*, a hemp-smelling store. It was short-sleeved, long and billowy, made from a crêpey material. But she would never wear something like that now. Now she wears a lot of brown, which she teams with black, white, green or rusty-red. No dresses, or hardly ever.

She's never been to the desert, though she'd like to go. Somewhere unearthly. She's never ridden a long way on a bus either. A train, yes. She rode on a train with her sister to New South Wales when they were quite young. To visit their Grandma. It was a ten-hour journey. At first they had wandered the carriages and poured themselves plastic-tasting water into cups, but later they just sat in their seats and took turns playing the Gameboy. Lots of long car-trips as well – North and West. There was a bend in the road on the way through the Adelaide hills called the Devil's Elbow, but that road's been redone and it's very straight and easy now.

When she writes, or before she writes, she feels herself coming up against a wall. A stupid image (just call it a Block and be done with it). Not like a brick wall, but a wall of hard air maybe, a clog in her throat, one of those painful hiccups. How to get past the blockage, she wonders, do I just start writing? She does, but it's so dull!

Her body? She only thinks of it occasionally. She doesn't think of it as 'carrying her through' or 'lumbering' along. Not yet, that's for later when you become grateful for anything. She's not grateful yet. She wishes her body was 'better', stronger and more flexible, leaner, more proportionate. Her problem is with her fingertips and heels. She picks at them and breaks skin away. It's a terrible habit, one she can't seem to shake. If she leans for too long on her heels they start to burn because they don't have that thick hard layer of skin heels are supposed to have.

Must she write of *beliefs?* She grew up in the church, the Reformed Church. She was asked from the pulpit what she would answer if God asked why she should be let into heaven. She knew the correct answer was *not* 'because I obeyed the commandments, because I helped the poor and sick, because I had faith and was good'. The answer was 'because you in your infinite wisdom have chosen to forgive me and grant me a place by your side'. And now? She still retains that image of finding a watch on the ground in the middle of nowhere.

Whose theory was that? St Anselm? Aquinas? She imagines one of those pocket watches on a chain, like Atticus Finch's. To find a watch before watches were invented; to find the world working like clockwork. And where the watchmaker?

When she writes she imagines, like the white-haired woman, people laughing at her. Breaking out into guffaws, or worse, sniggering secretly behind a polite hand. People who recognise the flimsiness of her arguments and her abysmal technique. People who have lived longer, read more, thought more complexities. And right they are, she thinks. Who is she, someone who went on a long train-ride and had a blue dress, to partake of this grand art? Who is she to slot herself alongside the names that glow from her bookshelves?

She has studied literature and knows a little of its history, or perhaps only a few of its modern transitions. When she was seven she wrote a story called 'Ouch!' about a visit to the optometrist and the consequent discovery of a pair of magical glasses. She became mildly famous for a day when she was asked to read the story to the Year 8 class, enormous lounging students, who looked at her strangely and clapped lazily at the end. She didn't know anything, then, about the meaning of story-telling. It was Frye, wasn't it, who wrote about the anxiety of influence? But what about an unpeopled literature? Literature without the massive figures themselves, no Homer, Shakespeare, Euripides, Tolstoy, Melville and so on? What of Literature the Law? She thinks of it as encounter, with no shaking hands or kissing cheeks. An encounter with two paces of separation. Like a magnet hovering above iron filings, moving them about without actual contact. An encounter, two facing different directions, each with their respective wills, propping up a wall.

She has met peers of hers who have told her how they write unstoppably, page after page, deep into the night so they don't realise the time, and all through the morning so they forget to eat. And she is shamed for the struggle it is for her to make a few messy lines, and then to knot the lines and bleed them dry and leave them there while she eats heartily and sleeps long. Of course she could not possibly be that real writer of the mad eyes and the odd clothes. At the supermarket she is careful to look for the bright yellow tags that indicate a special price. A real writer would never do this. A real writer would eat the mouldy bread and hard cheese they happened to find in the empty fridge. And while they ate, they would write.

She's also heard of the Muse, a willowy figure who whispers to real writers when their ideas dry up. It is the Muse, who is a goddess, that frenzies writers into their best works, who touches the living vein of art and prods it to the page. She used to go off alone, to places she thought the Muse might frequent, like the edges of rivers or windy beaches, but never felt the tap of the Muse on her shoulder. She put it down to self-consciousness. A real writer must be empty, like a Buddhist in meditation, and ready for the words to arrive. For some reason she's memorised a poem by Sir Thomas Browne that has the lines, 'Thou must empty all thyself of self / Like to a shell dishabited.' Although Browne was talking about letting the spirit of God enter, she knows it is the same for the real writer who must release the self and become a corridor through which stories pass like shadows.

Yet she still writes, though not a real writer. Far from a calling, it is a task – one she completes as best she can. All the while wondering what it is like on the other side where divine beings make their sinuous way through the open passageways of the great writers' minds.

Divided and Divined

Elizabeth Costello is the subject of many comparisons – metaphors and similes – within the book. She is a seal (Coetzee 2003a: 3), big cat (5), whale (6), a knight (7), a sibyl (30), zookeeper (32), python (34) and so on. Perhaps the most striking repeated image, as first observed by Elizabeth's son John, is the comparison between Costello and a god incarnated, "wheeled from village to village to be applauded, venerated" (31), or a god-human. This image is reintroduced, in different ways, in almost all of the eight lessons. In Lesson 8, the god-human divide is explored through the question of where Costello's "voices" come from, where the invisible of which she is 'secretary'. In the Animal chapters, the question is investigated in terms of philosophy and ethics: whether the distinction god/human/animal, is justified.

Elizabeth's son John, as one in a position to consider his mother over time both in her person and her writing, makes clear, in the first chapter, the double-sidedness of the writer: "I think you are baffled, even if you won't admit it, by the mystery of the divine in the human. You know there is something special about my mother – that is what draws you to her – yet when you meet her she turns out to be just another ordinary old woman. You can't square the two," (28).

Later, he provides a more visceral image of Costello as deeply flawed human:

> *This woman,* he would say if he were to speak, *whose words you hang on as if she were the sibyl, is the same woman who, forty years ago, hid day after day in her bedsitter in Hampstead, crying to herself, crawling out in the evenings into the foggy streets to buy the fish and chips on which she lived, falling asleep in her clothes. She is the same woman who later stormed around the house in Melbourne, hair flying in all directions, screaming at her children, 'You are killing me! You are tearing the flesh from my body!'* (30)

In Lesson 6, Elizabeth Costello encounters in Paul West another kind of juxtaposed divinity, this time 'an evil god' (159), 'the writer as duped by Satan' (*EC* 164). She relates her own brush with the devil, a sadistic beating at the hands of a docker with whom she refused to have sex, and compares the secret memory to an "egg of stone," and a "genie imprisoned in a bottle" (166-7). She finds her silence on the subject "good", "a silence she hopes to preserve to the grave" (166); (the passage reiterates the closeness of the third person to the thoughts of Elizabeth Costello, as the irony of her secret devil being now freed upon the world is completely disregarded.) Images of entry and re-lease, of a *transferral*, are central to the idea of the author divided and divine: "Through Hitler's hangman a devil entered Paul West, and in his book West in turn has given that devil his freedom, turned him loose upon the world" (167-8). However it is the often overlooked Lessons 5 and 7 which provide the most specific analysis of this particular aspect of the author divided.

The idea of the artist embodying and expressing the sublime is, by now, a matter of history.

> Can we *be one with* a god profoundly enough to apprehend, to *get a sense of,* a god's being?...it sounds to her a Kantian sort of question. If her ear is right, then inwardness started its run with the man from Königsberg and ended, more or less, with Wittgenstein the Viennese destroyer. (Coetzee 2003a: 187-88)

In *Gender and Genius*, Christine Battersby traces the term 'genius' through its transitions during the late 18th century, identifying it as an alternative to a fading faith in God: "Through their reverence for genius, even those thinkers who rejected God kept the essentials of the old Christian framework. Inside the human frame Christians had hidden an immortal 'soul'; now 'genius' was concealed within the chest of European man" (Battersby 1989: 3). It is the question of the union, the pocket of divine in human, which interests Costello, and which is pertinent to the question of the author divided. Battersby compares the pre-Romantic idea of the sublime with the idea of Romantic genius by contrasting the primitive nature-inspired aesthetics of Shakespeare to the "junior God-the-Father" law-giving aesthetics of Byron and Shelley. Whereas pre-Romantic aesthetics judged sublimity in terms of its effects on the audience, "overwhelming the spectator by a kind of mental rape," in Kant-influenced Romantic aesthetics "the emphasis was switched from the reactions of a passive spectator to the actions of the artistic producer" (75). In each case, the question of genius becomes one of transferral: in fact a highly sexualized question of entry and release, even without Battersby's specific gendered inquiry.

In the above quote, from Lesson 7 'Eros,' Costello is musing on 'inwardness,' and wondering why, in the various historical accounts of humans being descended upon by gods, those men and women never reflected upon or expressed their thoughts of the encounter. She thinks of Psyche, chosen by the god Eros to be his lover, whose story she has read retold by two American poets: Robert Duncan in 'Poem Beginning with a Line by Pindar' and Susan Mitchell in *Erotikon* (once again Coetzee does not shy away from naming real names): "*What about the girl,* she wants to ask the poet [Mitchell] – *if you can say what it was like for him, why not tell us how it was for her?*" (Coetzee 2003a: 184). The story of Anchises and Aphrodite also interests her, particularly how it was possible for Anchises, after "that signal night" to then live a normal human life: "he did not think overmuch about it, not as we understand thinking" (186). Mary of Nazareth is asked the same question: why struck dumb after the event, why not asked by her girlfriends, "*What was it like, how did it feel, how did you bear it?*" (187).

The question is a call to the imagination to broaden its range; it is writerly, almost journalistic. Elizabeth Costello wants to hear both sides of the story, both voices. It is her impulse to hear or experience and then to transfer the event into words and narrative. Coetzee, also the bearer of this impulse, allows Costello no hiding place, but proceeds, after she has concluded her lecture, or signed her letter, to tell the rest: her being beaten, her fellating an old man, her despairing, crying quietly, touching her withering body parts. The act of writing, for both, is the only way to understanding. As Coetzee says in an interview about Kafka: "No intensity of reading that I can imagine would succeed in guiding me through Kafka's verb-labyrinth: to do that I would once again have to take up the pen and, step by step, write my way after him" (Coetzee 1992: 199). In the same way, Costello is dissatisfied with the silence of the mortals and needs to write, even though it makes her blush, about "Mary of Nazareth's experience too, waking from her dream still slightly trembly with the issue of the Holy Ghost running down her thighs [...] *It must have been like being fucked by a whale...like being fucked by the Leviathan*," (Coetzee 2003a: 184, 187).

Another image of Mary appears within Elizabeth's long letter to her sister Blanche in Lesson 5. This time it is the image of Correggio's exuding mother Mary "who, secure in her virtue, boldly uncovers herself under the painter's gaze and thence under our gaze," (149). The image indicates again the intertwining of the divine and the erotic: "The atmosphere in the studio electric, but with what? Erotic energy? The penises of all those men, their *verges*, tingling? Undoubtedly. Yet something else in the air too. Worship...That heady mix of the ecstatic and the aesthetic," (150). It is that 'heady mix' which signals the third divide within the author and which concludes or consummates, as it were, the previous divides: the author both continuing towards death and transfixed in time; the author both particular and universal; the author both performing the arbitrary and partaking of the Law; and now the author both human and divine.

As Costello acknowledges, it is a Kantian question, this necessary combination of the beautiful and the sublime. In *Critique of Judgement*, Kant defines an aesthetical idea – with which he associates imagination, intuition and spirit – in contrast to ideas of reason:

> By an aesthetical idea I understand a representation of the imagination which occasions much thought, without however any definite thought, i.e. any *concept* being capable of being adequate to it; it consequently cannot be completely compared and made intelligible by language. We easily see that it is the counterpart (pendant) of a *rational idea*, which conversely is a concept to which no *intuition* (or representation of the imagination) can be adequate. (Kant 1914)

As Lewis Baldacchino interprets, Kant delineates the possibility or *appearance* of nature and art – as dependent on rules and forms such as grammar – from the possibility of its *beauty*: "The possibility of both art and nature, as conceived by Kant, depends on determinate concepts but the possibility of natural beauty as of beautiful art depends on indeterminate concepts" (Baldacchino 1991: 75). It is, however, necessary for both the formally familiar sensory image and the inaudible, inexpressible spirit to be present for a work to have that "animating effect on the mind" that indicates the truly sublime.

David Lurie, Coetzee's protagonist in *Disgrace*, speaks of the same interrelation in a class on Wordsworth's *The Prelude*. The image in the poem is Mont Blanc in the Alps, a stunning picture, but, as Lurie reads, a sense-image which usurps "the great archetypes of the mind, pure ideas." Lurie goes on to suggest that Wordsworth seeks a balance between the two:

> Not the pure idea, wreathed in clouds, nor the visual image burned on the retina, overwhelming and disappointing us with its matter-of-fact clarity, but the sense-image, kept as fleeting as possible, as a means toward stirring or activating the idea that lies buried more deeply in the soil of memory. (Coetzee 1999a: 22)

Images are also at the heart of *Slow Man* in Paul Rayment, a collector of antique photographs of Australia's mining history. In a beautifully wrought moment of connection between the ageing crippled Rayment and the youthful godlike Drago, it is a picture, in all its specificity, which holds the key to their commonality:

> Because just possibly this image before them, this distribution of particles of silver that records the way the sunlight fell, one day in 1855, on the faces of two long-dead Irishwomen, an image in whose making he, the little boy from Lourdes, had no part and in which Drago, son of Dubrovnik, has had no part either, may, like a mystical charm – *I was here, I lived, I suffered* – have the power to draw them together. (Coetzee 2005: 177)

The mystery is in the transferral of one moment through space – from Lourdes and Dubrovnik to Adelaide – and time, from 1855 to 2005, and, in a deeper sense, through layers of meaning and intellect to the buried soul itself and thence the connection of souls.

What power does the image, the still, have? Slavoj Žižek, in his book *The Sublime Object of Ideology*, extricates a definition of the sublime in Kant as a kind of failure: "The Sublime is an object in which we can experience this very impossibility, this permanent failure of the representation to reach after the Thing. Thus, by means of the very failure of representation, we can have a presentiment of the true dimension of the Thing" (1989: 203). Žižek goes on to contrast Kant's view of the Sublime as something existing "positively…beyond the field of representation, of phenomenality," thus consigning phenomenality to being a negative representation of the Thing, to Hegel's position that there is nothing beyond representation, that the Thing-in-itself exists within, not beyond, the experience of "radical negativity". At this point, another image from *Elizabeth Costello*'s Lesson 5 begins to assert itself, that of the carver of crucifixes, Joseph (that name most human among humans). "I saw Joseph's collection," Costello says to her sister. "A bit obsessive, wouldn't you call it? Just the same image, over and over again," (Coetzee 2003a: 136). Joseph's crucifixes are all the same: "The face of the tortured man is a formalized, simplified mask in a single plane, the eyes slits, the mouth heavy and drooping," (135). He stores boxes and boxes of them in his shed, has never carved anything else, and only arthritis stops him carving still more. To talk about the image itself, (and what an image – the man who is also God staked as a sacrificial lamb to repay the debts of humanity) in terms of Kant and Hegel is fairly uncomplicated. Kant, perhaps, would discuss the ultimate failure of the image, citing the Jewish Law in which he finds the commandment: Thou shalt not make unto thee any graven image, or any likeness of any thing that is in heaven or on earth, or under the earth, and so forth. (Kant 1914) However, inasmuch as the image "expands the soul" through its very inability to represent the enormity of its meaning, its failure, its solid sensory failure, is necessary. Hegel, on the other hand, would perhaps call the image an articulation of his so-called "infinite judgement," a "judgement in which subject and predicate are radically incompatible, incomparable: 'The Spirit is a *bone*', '*Wealth* is the Self', 'the State is *Monarch*', 'God is *Christ*'" (Žižek 1989:207). Thus the Nothing that Hegel finds when he looks behind phenomena is embodied in, as Žižek puts it, "some miserable, radically contingent corporeal leftover" (207). The object – here Joseph's small wooden cross – gives body to the absolute negativity of the Idea.

More difficult, however, is a discussion of the person who crafted the object – the artist. What is the image, the artwork, for them? Where did it come from? What is beyond it? For Correggio, Wordsworth, Fauchery and Joseph what is the artwork, where does it go, what does it do? Can one talk so philosophically about the makers of images? Coetzee poses questions like these in his presentation of the author-character in *Elizabeth Costello* and *Slow Man*, by making the artist herself an image to be contemplated: "She is panting: a woman in her sixties…wearing a floral silk dress cut low behind to reveal unattractively freckled, somewhat fleshy shoulders" (Coetzee 2005: 80). An image both startlingly corporeal:

> His hand tightens on his crutch. If it were a proper old-fashioned crutch of ash or jarrah…he would bring it down on the old hag's skull, again and again, as often as might be necessary, till she lay dead at his feet and her blood soaked the carpet. (89)

And somehow otherworldly:

> For an instant, for an aeon, time stops; one tumbles down a dark hole. Then, hey presto, one emerges into a second world *identical with the first*, where time resumes and the actions pro-ceeds…except that one now has Elizabeth Costello around one's neck, or someone like her. (122)

It is an image, and these are the questions, which one is invited, it seems, to ask about Coetzee himself, since he is the author behind the author-figure. We are told in newspaper profiles that Coetzee is a re-cluse, intensely private, abrupt with journalists who ask the wrong questions. Yet it could be argued that each of his novels is deeply con-fessional, deeply personal. It has been reported, for instance, that Co-etzee had a son who died in similarly mysterious circumstances, and in a similar fashion – by falling from a height – as Pavel, Dosto-evsky's stepson, did in Coetzee's novel *The Master of Petersburg*. Where else can an author address such a personal loss but in the dis-embodiment, the divide, of the moment of putting pen to paper? The chill omniscience of voice, the bodily pain of the human. In his later novels, the ones that have reviewers harking back to the 'glory days' of *Disgrace* and *Life and Times of Michael K*, Coetzee is drawing out the 'I,' as Paul Rayment puts it, "trapped behind the glass whose stare we are normally so careful to avoid. *Behold this being who eats with me, spends nights with me, says "I" on my behalf!...* Every now and then the stranger who says "I" breaks through the glass and speaks in me" (Coetzee 2005: 210).

Perhaps we consider the philosophy of art in the wrong terms. The image, as Rayment discovers, is not, as he once thought, "fixed, immutable" (64), but is more like a story, able to change shape and import according to its user, its new artist. The spark of the divine that can travel, quick as a flash, from writer to paper to reader, locks together with, becomes half of, its specific human user to form a new impression altogether. Whatever is beyond the human, beyond that guarded gate – the Law of literature, the mysterious unnameable Beauty – would remain silent and invisible were it not for the specific human lives and voices of its authors. Just as Coetzee's own person and life would remain hidden were it not for the extraordinariness of the form of art. In books like *Elizabeth Costello* and *Slow Man*, we the reader, the new artist, are invited to not just participate in but observe this strange combination – the gods who envy mortality, the humans who envy the divine – together, sometimes awkwardly, sometimes exasperatingly.

'A going against': Coetzee, postmodernism, and late style

Many reviewers of the novel *Slow Man* have criticised Coetzee for a perceived stinginess and over-control. As Sarah Emily Miano writes in *The Times*, "Coetzee offers his readers certain fictional possibilities and then denies them" (Miano 2005). Or as D J Taylor comments on the "horribly oblique" novel, "Coetzee insist[s] on the reader being left to do all the work" (Taylor, D. 2005). Almost all mention 'up to page 80' or 'the first third'[5] as being characteristic of Coetzee's compelling excellence with prose, and the rest as being a "conceit," a "code," "punctured," "twee," and above all, "implausible" and "distancing". The argument could certainly be made that Coetzee's latest two books were written with himself in mind, and therefore do not make that imaginative leap beyond the self – that leap that forges a space where writer and reader may meet on common, or in fact neu-

---

[5] It is perhaps interesting to note that the appearance of Elizabeth Costello comes at Chapter 13, something no reviewer has yet mentioned. Chapter 13 was also when John Fowles 'entered' his novel *The French Lieutenant's Woman*.

tral, ground. Since Coetzee seems to be his own ideal reader here, other readers will perhaps connect with the books to the extent that they are like Coetzee – writers, for example, may engage with the books more than non-writers. It is this element which reviewers seem to resist – a lack of generosity, an exclusion. The reader is asked to travel all the way back to the author in order to understand the text, where usually a character and plot meets them in the middle ground between observation and imagination.

Underlying reviewers' collective resistance seems to be an understanding of what does and does not belong in the novel today. In his review, Andrew Miller writes that upon the appearance of Elizabeth Costello, "the reader may emit an audible groan – she is Rayment's creator and he but a character in one of her stories" (Miller 2005: 32). One assumes that the groan is born not just out of a frustration, as Miller has it, in the "puncture, and the hiss of escaping drama, of novelistic vigour and invention," but out of a feeling that literature has already been through this, like a childish phase, and has come out the other end, once again seeking 'plausibility'. Benjamin Markovits writes in his review, "Such devices have long since lost the power to shock and their power to amuse is following hard behind" (Markovits 2005: 2). This fairly contemporary sentiment of literature needing to move beyond the lingering devices of a postmodern era sometimes shows itself to be a shallow one. Although academic texts seem yet to address the subject closely, there is certainly a climate, or 'sea change' as Robert McLaughlin puts it in his article on "Post-postmodern discontent," amongst the literary community that to (re)use language-play and authorial self-consciousness is not only an aesthetic step backward, but a refusal of the social responsibility of literature. A useful example is the critical response to Salman Rushdie's novel *Shalimar the Clown*. Rushdie, who as Peter Craven puts it is "like the Commonwealth's revenge on Gabriel García Márquez" (Craven 2005: 5), has a distinctive style of magic realism that toys with the historical event. But is his iconic style 'getting old'? In her review of *Shalimar*, Delia Falconer asks, "Are his novels doomed to repeat this same trick [of 'promiscuously multiplying narratives'] over and over?" and later comments, "Rushdie can't help himself. His book soon slips into the warm bath of cartoonish cliché and gratuitous cleverness" (Falconer 2005: 57-8). Craven echoes, "*Shalimar the Clown* is the latest instalment in his concerted attempt to turn himself into a cliché called Salman Rushdie." It is 'gratuitous' that is most telling here: the implication that a real tragedy (the disputed province of Kashmir) and real humanity, is overwhelmed, cheapened and subsumed by unnecessary prose, and cheeky self-reference.

McLaughlin resists a narrow assessment of postmodern fiction by rereading three of John Barth's seminal essays, particularly 'The Literature of Exhaustion' from 1967, and also two essays from the 1980s in which the original is defended and clarified. McLaughlin finds in the essays a confirmation that postmodern fiction is intended neither as "a dead end for language nor a severing of the referential relationship between language and literature and the world," but, quoting from Barth's 1988 'Postmodernism Revisited', is the only way of writing that "avoided false innocence…[and] said clearly that it is no longer possible to speak innocently" (McLaughlin 2004: 58).[6] He concludes by exhorting young writers – inheritors and disparagers of postmodernist techniques – to emphasize the representation of the world 'we all more or less share,' but in doing so, "to show that it's a world that we know through language and layers of representation; language, narrative, and the processes of representation are the only means that we have to experience and know the world, ourselves, and our possibilities for being human" (McLaughlin 2004: 67). With reference to such sentiments, Coetzee's *Slow Man* could be viewed as going against the tide of this 'sea-change' of re-emphasis on the plausibility of a shared world and the important real work of representation. Why now? one might ask, since Coetzee, during the height of postmodern playfulness in the 1980s was writing his political masterpieces, *Waiting for the Barbarians*, *Life and Times of Michael K*, and *White Writing*. Although these books referred latently to the self and to literature, that particular postmodern voice of excess and amusement remained absent. Here in *Elizabeth Costello* and *Slow Man*, the 'play' of author and character is a highly distressed one, jarring uncomfortably against attempts at categorisation.

Edward Said, writing with reference to Theodor Adorno's 1937 essay 'Late Style in Beethoven,' addresses the new idiom of the author writing late in life in his 'Thoughts on Late Style,' an essay fragment published in *The London Review of Books* in 2004. Rather

---

[6] McLaughlin here cites John Barth's 1988 'Postmodernism Revisited' in *Review of Contemporary Fiction* 8.3: 22.

than late works expressing a spirit of "reconciliation and serenity…a miraculous transfiguration of reality," as in Shakespeare's, Sophocles' and Verdi's final works, Said is interested in those late works that exhibit a "deliberately unproductive productiveness, a going against" (Said 2004: 3). As Adorno points out in the original article, often this tonal change is explained by art theorists as an arrival at subjectivity: "Studies of very late Beethoven seldom fail to make reference to biography and fate. It is as if, confronted with the dignity of human death, the theory of art were to divest itself of its rights and abdicate in favour of reality" (Adorno 1993: 103). However, as Adorno goes on to write, this explanation on its own is unsatisfactory: "In no case can the cliché 'subjective' be applied flatly to his stance. For, in general, in Beethoven's music, subjectivity – in the full sense given to it by Kant – acts not so much by breaking through form, as rather, more fundamentally, by creating it" (105). One can see how the cliché came about: when theorists are faced with a work by an ageing artist and see a preoccupation with death plainly in that work, the presumption of a pre-eminent subjectivity is understandable. Certainly in *Elizabeth Costello* and *Slow Man*, images of the body, its decay and death, abound, as in one of the most raw moments of the former:

> She turns on him a tearful face. What does she want, he thinks? Does she want me to answer her question for her?
> They are not yet on the expressway. He pulls the car over, switches off the engine, takes his mother in his arms. He inhales the smell of cold cream, of old flesh. 'There, there,' he whispers in her ear. 'There, there. It will soon be over.' (Coetzee 2003a: 115)

At sixty-five, there is no doubt that Coetzee has more years and probably more books still to come; but having won two Bookers, the Jerusalem Prize and the Nobel Prize, there is little left for him to achieve in terms of literary accolades. This particular subjectivity, however, perhaps one of rebellion or anachronism as Said has it, is not the sole informer of Coetzee's late works. Rather, the objective nature of impeccable and original form, and the subjective that "inhabit[s] the late works as a lamenting personality," (Said 2004: 3) co-exist. Adorno, on Beethoven, puts it superbly:

> Objective is the fractured landscape, subjective the light in which
> – alone – it glows into life. He does not bring about their harmo-

> nious synthesis. As the power of dissociation, he tears them apart
> in time, in order, perhaps, to preserve them for the eternal. In the
> history of art late works are the catastrophes. (Adorno: 1993: 107)

As catastrophes, then, *Elizabeth Costello* and *Slow Man* refer unfashionably to death, God, and the relationship between author and character. Georges Poulet, in his seminal article 'Phenomenology of Reading,' also reaches a now unfashionable conclusion to his discussion of "a critical method having as guiding principle the relation between subject and object" (Poulet 1969: 67). Again, it is *the image* that guides Poulet to a final recognition of the work's power existing in its formal absence, as he gazes at the masterpieces of the painter Tintoretto:

> I had suddenly the impression of having reached the common es-
> sence present in all the works of a great master, an essence which
> I was not able to perceive, except when emptying my mind of all
> the particular images created by the artist. I became aware of a
> subjective power at work in all these pictures, and yet never so
> clearly understood by my mind as when I had forgotten all their
> particular figurations. (68)

And what is this essence? Poulet cannot explain, but acknowledges, "that all subjective activity present in a literary work is not entirely explained by its relationship with forms and objects within the work…it is exposed in its ineffability." Coetzee's figuring of the author as both human and divine, able to transfer both a fragile honest history and the formless essence of subjectivity, has been, I argue, a career-long one. It is in his two late works, their unsettled and unsettling style, that the figuring steps bodily through the door in the disruptive character of Elizabeth Costello: she is a person and a metaphor, both a woman and a god.

*

2005

Elizabeth was almost finished reading J. M. Coetzee's new book *Slow Man*.

This time it had not caught her eye in a bookshop because it was not yet on the shelf; it was, in fact, still out in a back room, boxed, underneath other boxes. She had asked after it, as though it were a sick relative, and the storeperson, delighted, had gone to rummage out the back. Once it was in her hand, Elizabeth had asked, 'How much?' and the storeperson had said, 'Forty-five dollars,' apologetically. Rather than get the woman to go back to the box and replace the book, Elizabeth had bought it and the woman had said, opening the till, 'I'm sure it will be worth it,' with that special smile booklovers give to other booklovers in an inner-city chain bookstore.

Having already read eight reviews of the book, Elizabeth knew almost exactly what to expect as she began reading outside in the new September sunshine. She remembered, with that sudden flash one has when a physical sensation can be so clearly linked to a mental one, the pain she had been in whilst reading *Disgrace*, now more than a year ago. Since then, having begun taking the Pill, her times of menstruation had been hardly noticeable on the physical horizon. In fact, she was bleeding now, and still perfectly comfortable, mobile, alert. Perhaps not running along the beach in a bikini, as they did on the sanitary products advertisements, but still, out here, relaxed, without a sick bowl by her side and a sickly smell wafting around a close room.

The forty-five dollar book she held carefully, having removed the delicate dust-jacket and placed it out of reach of the kitten. She turned the pages without cracking the spine, wetting or bending the paper. When she could, she used both hands to hold it. As a bookmark she was using the pamphlet on changing one's name she had ordered from the Registry of Births, Deaths and Marriages. Who can change their name? ran one of the Frequently Asked Questions. Why do people change their names? Do I need to apply for a name-change when I get married? I am a child – can I change my name? The procedure seemed fairly straightforward. You simply filled in a form, signed it under the eyes of a Registry official, provided authorised copies of four kinds of identification, handed over the fee and that was that. Within fifteen business days, you were known as something else.

There was a note beside the section 'Reason for changing your name': *Reason MUST be specific eg 'personal' is NOT acceptable*. Elizabeth thought most reasons for changing one's name would be personal. One's name is personal. Of course, she had heard of those people, probably Americans, who changed their name every couple of years as though it were a hair colour. To them, perhaps, the change was not so personal, more fancy or *whimsy*. To her, the reason for the

change went back twenty-three years to her birth when her father, perhaps muddled, perhaps shaking with the strain of birth-watching, had
entered *Elizabeth Katherine* as his new daughter's Given Names.
They were the names, of course, on which he and his wife had decided, sitting in the lounge during the Adelaide winter as the baby
filled out, grew rotund. 'Wouldn't it be lovely,' his wife might have
said, 'if she were to have names from our mothers, family names.
Your mother's middle name and my mother's middle name. Names
that go back into the minds of other mothers in Holland and Scotland.
Names that repeat.' And so it was decided. But the spelling of his
mother-in-law's middle name was not something Elizabeth's father
had thought to check, so *Katherine* he put, and it stayed.

She, Elizabeth, had gone back to Adelaide recently for a sad
event: her Oma, her mother's mother, had died and was to be buried
alongside her husband in Enfield Cemetery. She thinks 'a sad event,'
and it was certainly sad: that signal passage from John's gospel that
was read at the graveside, 'In my father's house are many rooms. I am
going there to prepare a place for you so that you can be there where I
am.' And the memories her Aunts and Uncles had of their mother, the
smells and tastes. The eloquence of their eulogies (which they must
have written in the early hours, in haste). A sad event, but for her, not
such a personal one. She had moved from Adelaide at nine years and
had only seen her Oma two or three times since, retained only vague
images of elbow macaroni, woodworking tools, cigarettes and binocu-
lars for bird-watching. When all the family had gathered for her Opa's
funeral the year before, Oma had seemed disoriented and fussy more
than anything. In the middle of the gathering at her flat post-
ceremony, she'd said she was tired and wanted everyone to leave.
Oma had kissed Elizabeth vaguely as though she wasn't really sure
which grand-daughter this towering young woman was.

Oma's parents had liked the four Cs of the name they chose:
Christina Catherina Charlotta Clement. Oma had since replaced the
flamboyant 'a' endings with e's and it was the Catherine which Elizabeth's parents had picked out for their daughter. So all these processes
for a single letter in the end: *K* to *C*. She would have to call the bank
and the people who issued driver's licenses and tell them: I've made a
slight change to my middle name, will I need to have my identification reprinted? She'd already practised using the EC in a signature,

finding any join between the two initials awkward, and in the end leaving them separate.

She is aware of the strange coincidence of the name, the *confluence* of Elizabeths and ECs. They seem to lie in wait for her like mischief-makers. Coetzee's other book about an old woman, *Age of Iron*, had Elizabeth Curren dying of breast cancer. Breast cancer ran in her, Elizabeth Catherine's, family – in fact her grandmother, her father's mother (Adelaide Elizabeth), had survived it ten years ago. A coincidence like this she bore, as a good reader must, with even humour, without sulking. Elizabeth Chandos's letter she has already addressed and has dealt with (*I am not mad*) the coincidences springing from it: the date of her birthday, the dream about New York. And Elizabeth Costello herself, whose appearance in this new book has reviewers up in arms, seems to be meddling, from wherever she lives in Carlton, Melbourne (*just down the road!*), her puppeteering arms securely into her life.

She continues reading from where she left off and finds Elizabeth Costello telling Paul Rayment, the book's hero, a story. Sinbad helps an old man across a river by carrying him on his shoulders. When they reach the other side, the old man, instead of climbing down, starts choking Sinbad by tightening his legs around Sinbad's throat. 'Now you are my slave who must do my bidding in all things,' says the old man, (says Elizabeth Costello, says J. M. Coetzee). Somehow the image, in its grotesquerie, all its tactile coarseness – *the withered skin of the thighs, the loincloth, the leer* – enters her imagination beyond the call of the book's intention. The two of them grappling at the river's edge, the old man (or woman, as it is now suggested) perhaps gripping the young man's head, covering his eyes, tugging his hair; riding him as he teeters about, flails blindly, hits at her legs, tosses his torso to try to lose her. The two of them, now resigned, continuing on past the water, becoming like one body, she pointing the way, he feeding her morsels. She, Elizabeth, sees the image coming out at her from all directions, the positions and characters swapping: Sinbad and the old man, Paul Rayment and Elizabeth Costello, Elizabeth Costello and J. M. Coetzee. It is an image, and like all images it fails. Not a deadening failure, not really a loss; that beautiful failure that reaches endlessly for what it knows is there: the end, realisation, God.

Where is Coetzee? Authors and Characters.

Coetzee's connection with Daniel Defoe's *Robinson Crusoe* is recognized from his 1986 book *Foe*, from his essay which appears as the introduction to the *World Classics* edition of *Crusoe*, and more recently from his remarkable 2003 Nobel prize lecture 'He and His Man'. Before reading the lecture proper, Coetzee, by way of introduction, remarked on his boyhood impression of the connection between Robinson Crusoe and Daniel Defoe:

> I read with the fullest attention this story, the story of the desert island that is turned into an island kingdom. Robinson Crusoe became a figure in my imagination. So I was puzzled when, some months later, I came across a statement in the Children's Encyclopaedia to the effect that someone else besides Robinson Crusoe and Friday was part of the island story: a man with a wig called Daniel Defoe... The encyclopaedia referred to the man as the author of *Robinson Crusoe*, but this made no sense since it says on the very first page of *Robinson Crusoe* that Robinson Crusoe told the story himself. Who was Daniel Defoe? What had he done to get into the Children's Encyclopaedia along with Robinson Crusoe? Was Daniel Defoe perhaps another name for Robinson Crusoe? An alias that he used when he returned to England from his island and put on a wig? (Coetzee 2003c)

Towards the end of the lecture, Coetzee asks what the relationship is to be between he (Robin Crusoe as he is called here) and his man (whom one assumes is Defoe): "How are they to be figured, this man and he? As master and slave? As brothers, twin brothers? As comrades in arms? Or as enemies, foes? What name shall he give this nameless fellow with whom he shares his evenings and sometimes his nights too?" (Coetzee 2003c). In *Elizabeth Costello,* and even more plainly in *Slow Man*, the barrier that usually separates author from character, by various devices such as voice, setting and narration, is deliberately blurred. As my colleague asked of the books, 'Where is Coetzee?' Where does he position himself, from which location is he speaking, how close is he, in fact, to the opinions and personality of his protagonist?

The reader is never given the chance to see any part of Costello's great works of fiction, to which her status as a celebrity-author is attributed. We cannot tell how transparent she has made herself when writing, for instance, the character of Molly Bloom in *The House on Eccles Street*. What we do have is a work of fiction by J. M.

Coetzee, another author who, because of one or two very famous works, has become something of a celebrity. David Lodge lists a few of the "teasing similarities and differences between [Costello] and her creator": their connection to Australia: Costello's birthplace, Coetzee's part-time home; their 'borrowing' from another work for their own fiction: for Costello *Ulysses*, for Coetzee *Robinson Crusoe* (Lodge 2003). He could easily have added any of the following doublings: "She has been married twice," (Coetzee 2003a: 1); she made her name with her fourth novel (Coetzee's *Michael K*); "She is by no means a comforting writer," (5); she is sometimes treated as "a Mickey Mouse post-colonial writer," (9); she is often asked the stock question about whether she finds it easy writing from the position of the opposite sex (12); she is a vegetarian and concerned with the place of animals in society (Ch. 3 & 4); she has written a liberal paper on censorship (160; Coetzee's *Giving Offense: Essays on Censorship*). All this apart from the (sometimes literally blindingly obvious) fact that they have each given the same lectures, read the same words from the page, one simply a certain remove away.

In *Slow Man* the principal trait of Costello's which relates directly to her 'author-ness' is a frightening coldness. As Paul Rayment becomes more and more agitated with her presence and her interfering ways, he is time and again repelled by Costello's assumption of control:

> 'Wouldn't you find it easier to use someone who came to you more willingly?' he remarks as dryly as he can. 'Give up on me. I am not an amenable subject.'[…]
>
> 'And your unsuitable passion? Where would I find another such?'
>
> 'My passion, as you call it, is none of your business, Mrs Costello.'
> She gives a wintry smile, shakes her head. 'It is not for you to tell me my business,' she replies softly. (Coetzee 2005: 89)

After which Rayment, who considers himself a discrete being, and rightful proprietor of his own business, not an open subject, considers bashing the old hag to death. Is this cold, yet soft, even regretful, attitude also the one Coetzee must adopt when he writes the characters who, wilfully or not, come to him? And if so, what of his relationship to Costello, also an author who knows the stinging guilt and compulsion of the writer? Then again, the parallels between Rayment and

Coetzee are also in evidence: both living in Adelaide, South Australia after arriving from afar; both ageing, both bike-riding; both, perhaps, speaking words "selected, one after the other, from the word-box you carry around with you, and slotted into place. That is not how a true native speaks, one who is born into the language" (Coetzee 2005: 230). In any case, it is certainly apparent that the strange and shifty relations between author and character are again at the foreground of Coetzee's attention, enough for him to address them in the lecture which must ostensibly attend to the heart of literature itself.

Elizabeth Costello, on many occasions in both *Elizabeth Costello* and *Slow Man*, says that her characters "come to" her. As mentioned earlier, she calls herself a "secretary" to her characters, a phrase she has borrowed from Czeslaw Milosz's poem 'Secretaries':

> I am no more than a secretary of the invisible thing
> That is dictated to me and a few others.
> Secretaries, mutually unknown, we walk the earth
> Without much comprehension. Beginning a phrase in the middle
> Or ending it with a comma. And how it looks when completed
> Is not up to us to inquire, we won't read it anyway. (Milosz 1988: 343)

In the section 'A Moment of Rupture,' the phrase was used to highlight the divide between Costello as author and Costello as individual; Milosz's poem concerns the blankness, the de-specified nature of the secretary: she is record-keeper, listener, channel. She does not interact with her dictation. Milosz himself affirms his personal support for the words: "I strongly believe in the passivity of a poet, who receives every poem as a gift from his daimonion or, if you prefer, his Muse. He should be humble enough not to ascribe what is received to his own virtues" (Milosz 1988: 1). In Lesson 8, the two sides of the author, both impersonal and deeply personal, as figured in Elizabeth Costello are registered as a paradox. Now, however, I would like to examine the phrase with regard to the relationship between author and character, for in *Slow Man* Elizabeth Costello does not remain blank behind her desk, but emerges to tug and push at her invisible thing.

The novel *Foe*, almost entirely enclosed within the quotation marks of its narrator Susan Barton, also addresses the contradictory nature of the author. On the one hand, Susan muses, isn't it the fate of all storytellers to "exist as the one who came, the one who witnessed, the one who longed to be gone: a being without substance, a ghost beside the true body of Cruso" (Coetzee 1986a: 51). A secretary, in fact, 'Without much comprehension.' Yet on a number of occasions Susan also considers the necessity of intervention in order to make the story of her year as a castaway more interesting: "Dubiously I thought: Are these enough strange circumstances to make a story of? How long before I am driven to invent new and stranger circumstances?"(67) The same tension exists between Rayment and Costello: Rayment wishes to see himself as living a real life even when, perhaps, there is not much happening in it; Costello conceives 'strange circumstances,' like the encounter she organizes between Rayment and the blind woman Marianna, in order to push Paul from the 'sad decline' of his life since its dramatic opening with the accident (Coetzee 2005: 100). Costello is certainly not the passive 'receiver' she claims to be in Lesson 8. The readers of *Slow Man*, judging by the impression one receives from most reviews of the book, feel frustrated by the intrusion – by the presence of the meddling author they are forced to remember. The awareness, however, carries even further than the novel. As Rayment thinks to himself during his arranged coupling with Marianna: "In a certain sense they are being watched, he is sure of that, on the back of his neck he can feel it," and later imagines finding Elizabeth Costello "stretched out on the carpet like a dog, watching and waiting," (112). Those scenes in the book, then, in which Elizabeth Costello is absent, are still heavy with her implicit presence. The reader recalls the 'first third' and imagines Costello directing the traffic, motioning for Wayne Blight's car to enter *now*, and hurtle its way into the bones of Rayment's leg. The reader will perhaps recall *Disgrace* or *Waiting for the Barbarians* and wonder if there was once a figure like Costello interfering here and there before she was edited out.

Like a maths student credited with insight for using the right methods even when she doesn't arrive at the correct answer, Coetzee 'shows his workings,' reveals the cruel mechanics of the author; cruel both to the 'puppet,' as Rayment calls himself, and the puppeteer, who would rather sit back in her secretary's chair and wait for the next line to be dictated, like a 'true' artist. All these matters resound again with Coetzee's rediscovered boyhood confusion at the connection between Robinson Crusoe and Daniel Defoe. Those adventures which make such fanfare of being a 'true account,' actually contain the implicit presence of the scene-setter, Defoe, who darts in and out placing a cannibal here, a fire there, and retreats to watch how it plays out.

Foe, a book which could also be described as a dialogue between author and character, contains another significant connection with *Slow Man*: an exact replica of an image. The image of Costello as Sinbad's, or Rayment's, bane, her legs around his neck in a figure of authorial strangulation, is, almost exactly, (p)reinscribed in *Foe*. Susan calls it 'The old man of the river':

> There was once a fellow who took pity on an old man waiting at the riverside, and offered to carry him across. Having borne him safely through the flood, he knelt to set him on the other side. But the old man would not leave his shoulders: no, he tightened his knees about his deliverer's neck and beat him on his flanks and, to be short, turned him into a beast of burden. He took the very food from his mouth, and would have ridden him to death had he not saved himself by a ruse. (Coetzee 1986: 147-8)

Where in *Slow Man*, the beast of burden became a representation of the character, and his oppressor the author, Susan is here motioning herself and Friday, with the latter as "the tyrant riding on my shoulders." A deplorable assertion if one is reading the tongueless Friday, as most do, as "symbolic of the denial of (political) voice to black South Africans by white colonists" (Worthington 1996: 253).[7] Foe is quick to remind her, "If Friday had his tongue back he would claim the contrary." However the figurings are not so dissimilar as they at first seem. On a number of occasions in *Foe*, Friday is given the raiments and status of the book's (the book which *Foe* gestures towards) true, but silent, author. He dons Foe's robes and wig and is even mistaken for the famous author when he sits at the desk, "poised over Foe's papers, he held a quill with a drop of black ink glistening at its tip" (Coetzee 1986a: 151). In the mysterious section four, which critics have variously seen as the narration of Coetzee himself, a dreaming or insane Susan, or the readerly 'I,' it is clear that Friday's mouth, his voice, lie at the heart or "eye," as Foe calls it, of the story:

---

[7] See also Jane Gardam's review of *Foe* 'Books: the only story,' September 7 1986 in *The Sunday Times*.

> His mouth opens. From inside comes a slow stream, without
> breath, without interruption. It flows up through his body and out
> upon me; it passes through the cabin, through the wreck; washing
> the cliffs and shores of the island, it runs northward and south-
> ward to the ends of the earth. (Coetzee 1986a: 157)

So Susan's 'old man of the river' could perhaps be the twin of Rayment's Arabian Nights fable – Friday the true author with Susan, a
struggling character in her own poor monologue, beneath.

It is the shift, the transferral, between author and character
that is most interesting here. Friday was one of the first and most sub-
ordinate characters in the history of the novel, and is here rewritten as
the one who possesses true authorial power. Susan too, especially in
section three, wavers between being character and reluctant, confused
author of her own surroundings:

> I continue to describe and explain. Listen! I describe the dark
> staircase, the bare room, the curtained alcove, particulars a thou-
> sand times more familiar to you than to me; I tell of your looks
> and my looks, I relate your words and mine. Why do I speak, to
> whom do I speak, when there is no need to speak? (Coetzee
> 1986a: 133)

Elizabeth Costello also manifests and expands upon this shift. In a
remarkable passage in Chapter 20 of *Slow Man*, Paul finds the old
woman by the riverside sitting on a bench. As always, Elizabeth begins a long 'lesson' and Paul listens, irritated. In the end the lesson
seems to be one of symbiosis. She says:

> "*He finds her by the riverside, sitting on a bench, clustered
> around by ducks that she seems to be feeding* – it may be simple,
> as an account, its simplicity may even beguile one, but it is not
> good enough. It does not bring me to life. Bringing me to life may
> not be important to you, but it has the drawback of not bringing
> you to life either." (Coetzee 2005: 159)

For the first time here, the reader is presented with the intimation that
Rayment is also involved with the writing of the book. Costello has
flung words back at him, implying that as the chapter opened with
Rayment looking for and then finding Costello, he was also authoring
his actions, albeit with Costello acting as omniscient editor. According
to Costello, he must do his work better for she is fading away. Indeed

when Paul takes a closer look at her he finds her colourless, feature-less, she has lost weight and her face is pallid. He has not filled her, or fleshed her out, is the implication. The relationship that was supposed to be symbiotic has become unequal. Of course this new figuring of the two raises many questions, the most interesting here being Where is Coetzee? If the two characters have been transformed into each other's author, 'bringing each other to life,' where is the place for Coetzee? One can assume that on the other side of the creative pen, Coetzee is also being brought to life, created.

Looking again at Coetzee's previous works through the lens of these latest two, one finds that characters are often also figured as authors, and that relations between characters are often like those between an author and character. *Foe* makes the positions quite visible, but other relationships like that between Mrs Curren and Vercueil in *Age of Iron* and between the unnamed doctor and Michael(s) in *Michael K*, are characterised by a similar mutual projection. In other words, Mrs Curren and the doctor both project stories upon their quiet, obscure counterparts and in doing so discover more about their own narrative lives. Susan too, once she begins to write the story of Cruso and Friday, becomes increasingly aware of, though denies, the potential of her own life as an authored narrative. And thus with Paul Rayment, who with tentative lines begins to depict Costello as he sees her: *on a bench, clustered around by ducks*. As he does it seems he is becoming more reconciled with the idea of himself as character, able to be described and contained.

Once again the moment of putting pen to paper indicates a divide: the writer is at once author and character, creator and created. As one authors, so one becomes aware of oneself as character; and as one is authored, like Rayment, so one becomes more aware of one's potential to author. Examining again Rayment's sentence at the beginning of Chapter 20, with the knowledge of Coetzee's keenly linguistic mind, another familiar idea begins to surface. *In the end he finds her by the riverside, sitting on a bench, clustered around by ducks that she seems to be feeding*. There is something dizzying about the sentence; first *he* is the subject: the seeker, the finder. What he has found, though – his object – is only figured by her *sitting on a bench*, by the strangely passive *clustered around by ducks*. It is as though his eye, seeing riverside, bench, ducks, has foregone *she*, the central image, who becomes a kind of blur, outlined rather than depicted. The sentence falls awkwardly on *that*, its rhythm leading one to imagine a further description of the ducks, but instead is followed by *she seems to be feeding*: a hesitant, and inward, motioning toward the obscured figure of Costello. The familiar idea that surfaces from the sentence is that of the middle voice, as coined by Barthes and followed by Coetzee in his 'A Note on Writing'. Remembering that, as Coetzee has it, "the three voices active, middle, passive may then be thought of as a cautionary chorus always to be lent an ear when one is doing-writing" (Coetzee 1984b: 11), one can perhaps imagine them ringing around this sentence as it was formed. The middle voice has reference to the self, in fact *contains* the self as agent of writing; Rayment's awkward sentence that seems to demand a rereading immediately on its ending, indicates Rayment himself, struggling, deficient, evasive.

Her man and she

After J. M. Coetzee's 2003 Nobel lecture, 'He and his man,' and his 2003 book Elizabeth Costello.

Although she knows she shouldn't, she looks one day into the drawer that holds his diaries. He's away and won't be back for weeks, 'on the circuit,' as he calls it. Ten diaries, a solid pile, each a different colour and design. They are a yearly gift to himself, though to imagine him, in a gift store, choosing from among leather and cloth, A5 and A4, looking at price tags, makes her redden with shame for him. She selects the one from 1976. Thirty year old ink in faded writing-blocks on the page, each block numbered, unbroken into paragraphs or days. He is writing about a woman who he sees trapped in a lull, maddened by the sky and the dust, a purgatory in which everything but herself simply goes on existing. Despite the roaring of dream-violence, and despite the seizing of white by black, the crossing of stone barriers, still the heavy sky, the blistering sun, continue without breaking apart. The woman is a hazy figure among the mindscape, an outline, a sign. She, the reader, feels herself falling for the young white woman who, lusting and dirty, denies herself sex until it is forced upon her. In the diaries, there are short bursts of description, like reminiscence, annotated with questions: "What does a skirt do on one's thighs when one flops down in the dust beside a river?" and "How many times to repeat the rape? Is three times enough? Is four?"

She puts the diary down, ill-at-ease with her hurried trespassing, and wanders to his armchair by the fireplace. Next to it is a rosewood side-table on which books are piled, and his second pair of reading glasses. She settles in the chair and puts the glasses on her nose, picks up a book: the short stories of Franz Kafka. She tries to cast herself into the crevices of the chair and sits with her legs crossed, as he does. She scans the words on the page, tries to still her restless feet, holds her head cocked, her jaw unlocked and crooked.

Later, she roams through the empty rooms. In her hand is the diary from 1980. She opens the door to his study and the cat, who had been asleep on the rug, stirs and yawns. She picks it up, as she has seen him do, and nestles it under her chin, scratching its forehead. She sits at the desk and turns on the overhanging lamp. The pages of the diary are soft and complicated with the indentations of words. This time he writes in columns and doubles. *Colony, sunglasses, borders, purification ritual* on the one hand, *barbarian, the hut by the granary, scars, mute* on the other. Between the columns are question marks and connecting lines, *jurisdiction* travelling along one, *torture* along another. There seems to be a figure, M, that appears repeatedly, but she is unsure of his real quality since he appears on both sides of the columns. In the corner of the page is a little line drawing: a man standing by a pool of water watching an animal – a deer? – which stands stiff, one leg bent in the air. The drawing has been circled many times and there are various arrows coming from the columns which point to it. The page itself, though hectic with interlocking lines and repeated words, lies still and soft on her hand as her eyes trace the arrows and movements. She smooths the page with her hand – a noise like the letter *s*, lisped.

She wakes suddenly from a dream and finds herself still in the study, uncomfortable in a tall straight-backed chair, her head lolling onto her shoulder. She rises stiffly and returns the diary to its drawer. She had dreamt a fearsome figure, both man and woman, both terroriser and coward, enormous, containing many signals, holding time still, its words protruding like a limb from its mouth.

She sleeps in his bed, making herself small under the covers. When she wakes it is to the sound of a voice – his. She hears the last words of a message left on the answering machine, 'I will be back soon.' She gets up and goes to the mirror. With her eyes still bleary her face in the glass looks smeared, unformed.

It is a sunny morning and she takes the diary from 1983 outside to read. By now, she has lost any feeling of guilt. The diaries don't seem forbidden, but like invitations, openings; as she reads them it is as though she is treading a path already laid for her.

This diary is different again from the previous two. There are only a few words on each unlined page, the rest is left blank. Sometimes the words are in the centre of the page, large and thick, as though formed slowly and heavily. Sometimes the words are in his usual tight script. It is as though there were two people here, working on the diary side by side. *I sit here day after day*, one of the large entries goes, *I don't need to eat. I can be still as a rock.* She reads the scripted entry on the next page; the handwriting is skewed as though written in haste: *A curse on it all! I am the law-enforcement, I am the boot in the head, I am the kick in the backside. I am the peering eyes of strangers and the pitying arms of women. I will take this from him at any cost. I will take the words from his mouth along with his food and his entrails.* The rest of the page is blank and crumpled.

As she reads the diary, which now seems to her like a two-handed duel, the sun shines on her face, warming her shoulders and beaming on the page of the book until it gleams. She reads this diary slowly, absorbing it, just as the pores of her skin are opening and drinking in the sun's heat. Coming inside in the evening, the bright page is still emblazoned across her vision. She feels heavier, shiny with sweat, and must stoop drunkenly to enter the low bedroom doorway.

In the morning her bones ache, her gums feel swollen and sore. She has a headache behind her eyes. She looks in his cupboards and finds a bottle of whiskey, adds a shotglass-full to her coffee and tops it with cream and icing-sugar, a combination of tastes she feels is just right.

Knowing she doesn't have much time left, she skips ahead and selects the diary from 1990. This one is not contained in a bound book, but is a sheaf of papers folded into a blank envelope. As she reads, she feels her heart beating faster. Her man writes, this time, of an old woman. He writes with affection and sadness. He sees her, he writes, wherever he looks – resting in his bed, walking past him in the street, her face at his window at night. *She is here with me on the page, her fingers inhabiting mine.* In the woman's life is another presence, a simple quiet one like the heavy-handed pages from the 1983 diary. It is towards this obscure trackless company that her life begins to tilt, or at least be edged by. Somehow, despite their differences, she the epistolary he the messenger, they seal each other's fissures, replace the parts that have been severed under knife or law. She, the reader, quivers at his descriptions of the dying woman's fears for her safety: *Like some wingless ineffectual bird, locked in her cage, the last of the dodos, old, past egg-laying, 'Now you are safe,' the zookeeper whispers.* As she reads, there is something that sets her trembling: a name, a voice, a premonition. This old woman and her story, in the meditative words of her man, stirs something, like the stirring of dividing cells, inside her.

She receives a postcard from him dated seven days ago. *I am thinking of you,* he writes, *as I do the rounds and tout old rituals of speech.* She smiles and swells. The picture on the front is of a grand old building surrounded by greenery and the wafting shadows of young people. Just as she had imagined it.

He will be arriving tomorrow. She moves on to the diary from 1994 and starts to skim it hurriedly, but then pauses to take in what she is reading. On the left hand side of the page is the running account of another man's life: date of birth, parents' backgrounds, youth, major events, sicknesses, work. On the right side are reflections on death her man has written carefully, tightly spaced. This page, as are all the right-hand pages she flicks through, is smudged with tearstains. *Does he, D, feel this too? The return to storytelling like a piston-engine, inescapable, locked into this motion of hand across page, of one word built atop another?* Later, as the notes and quotations pertaining to the other man become more and more detailed and minute, the right-hand pages become almost unintelligible, scrawled nonsense words that dip across the page like death throes. *Water in the beard*, goes one, *a child in the bed, I'd sell my soul, I'd mistreat that child, to write, to write, to write...*

She puts down the diary, shuddering. She feels suddenly very tired and afraid. Lately, though she has tried to refuse it, she has begun to hear sounds that aren't really there. Waking in the night she might hear a thud and then a whispered voice. Visions then spring through her mind – what the sounds might mean, who might be invading the house. And then, more dreadful still, come the words she might use to tell the story of the invasion, the rape, the violence. And then there is he, her man, whose presence she feels everywhere. Sometimes she has the eerie feeling that he is still here in the house, hiding during the day and emerging at night; shifting objects so they are in easier reach, moving others to the back, planning her movements, forging some subtle course for her. Even the diaries have been placed to be seen and reached for. Especially the diaries.

She checks her watch and finds it is already evening. She shivers. Even the hours and the minutes pass swiftly or sluggishly according to the will of her man. She is suddenly distracted by the sight of her own hand, held in a fist, the wrist bent. Ropy blue veins wind like canals, bunching the skin into clumps and rifts. Her knuckles are wizened hills surrounded by moats of spongy flesh. When did this happen? She cannot remember the transition; she cannot remember a time when her flesh was taut. Or rather, she can call up certain episodes of her youth clearly, in unmistakable detail, but to try and recall her hand, before it collapsed like this… There is nothing, a blank, a shadow-hand.

She finds she is shaking and rises, walks over to the drawer of diaries as though her legs are being lifted, her feet placed one before the other. She takes the last three diaries, dated 1997, 1999 and 2001 and sits once again in his armchair. This time she does not even try to affect his poses, but relaxes into his position easily. She reads like a robot, barely moving, her eyes scanning the words like a preset precision weapon, bullets or lasers firing at precise targets according to a code. She reads pages at random, first from one diary, then another, becoming confused as to who is who, what is what. At one point she finds herself reading notes for another character, but one who is so similar to he himself, to her man, that she begins to wonder if perhaps he did not write these diaries at all, but someone else. Another person with him in mind. Could it be possible, and she does not stop the thought as it comes like a missile through her mind, that it was in fact *she* who, in a trance perhaps, has written these diaries? Written them and then read them in that voice she knows so well, which she seems to hear her own thoughts in: his?

It is at this point that she hears a key being turned in the lock of the front door. Footsteps and the creak of luggage approach. She has not even noticed the night passing and the new day beginning. It is today, the day of his arrival. She stands up from the chair, letting the diaries fall to the floor.

Although they are only paces apart, he in the doorway, she standing before the armchair, it is as though a ravine has broken open between them, or a torrent. It is difficult for her to make him out, so blurred has her vision become, and so loud the roaring of blood in her ears. He is saying something about his trip, about the talks he has given all over the globe these past weeks. He has been asked, he says, many difficult questions by those in attendance, and sometimes has had no satisfactory answer to offer. She tries to understand what he is suggesting, but the sound of his voice and that pitching water between them have become thunderous. People seem to expect something else from him, he is saying, because of who he is. He begins to walk forward now, into the shallows. What would you say, he asks now, if I were to introduce you to the world? If it were you to whom they were directing their questions? She is trembling again; she needs to get out, past him to the door and then out onto the street. My emissary, he is saying as he advances, a stranger to them, but no stranger to their ways. She is desperate to get out, the only way is past him, and the gulf between them. He falls suddenly to his knees and lets out a sound, a low *oof*. She moves instinctively to help him, but he sinks further until he is prostrate on the floor. It is her only chance at crossing and she takes it, putting first one foot and then the other onto his back. She needs to apologise; opens her mouth, takes a breath.

*

The Ethics of Embodiment

Having examined the various ways in which the moment of writing signals a split within the author, attention will now be turned towards what is being written: from the mark to the line to the word, to the sentence, to meaning. I have been asking of Coetzee's author figures: what happens to someone when they write? Now I want to ask: why do they write at all, and what do they write of? To put it another way, it is the difference between the act, and the reflection upon the act; or in Coetzee's parlance between 'to write' and 'to *do* writing.'

Lesson 6 of *Elizabeth Costello* is a confronting piece of literature; it confronts one from many angles. The reader is harrowed by the central question of Costello's argument: are there some things – events, acts, scenes – that 'do not belong in the light of day,' so should remain buried? The reader is harrowed again by Costello herself, and the revelation of her own experience with 'evil'; disturbed further by the presence of real-life author Paul West: his stony silence, his still profile. Once again, questions that appear abstract: 'Why write?' are complicated by Coetzee as he steadies them with questions of specificity and individuality. Costello is arguing a point that must have philosophical and universal significance, but the reader cannot avoid the presence of her aging body, her dry mouth, and her grim memories. So it is in the context of this echoing divide between Costello as mouthpiece and Costello as individual, that the question of the value of art, or specifically literature, arises.

It is a question asked by philosophers throughout the ages, and in the modern age asked specifically with regard to literature post-World War II. The question inevitably becomes bound up in questions of the nature of truth, especially as we see more and more cases of authors coming under public recrimination for publishing what is ostensibly fiction under that tenuous category, 'autobiography'. Is the truth in fact more valuable than fiction? What can literature offer that is helpful in a society where 'help' is often a practical and mediated process of donation or sponsorship? What are the responsibilities of today's authors: to expose the deeper truths that lie beneath cut-and-paste journalism? to thus edify readers, and allow them to fulfil their obligation of knowledge or remembrance? Or is it rather to present an alternative: is the author's responsibility, rather, to literature, to imagination, to sound and pace, rhythm and texture, to art? On what terms is literature judged, what are the values assigned to it? And how does an author, that figure both single and universal, feel the weight of these values, judgements and responsibilities? Elizabeth Costello, for one, is bowed down by them, and sometimes defeated.

This section will again address the larger issue of the value of literature in the context of Coetzee's work with a focus on his two latest novels. All of Coetzee's numerous author-figures are highly concerned with the greater sufferings in the world and all feel guilt as they continue 'indulging' in a practice that commentates rather than addresses or solves. At the end of *The Master of Petersburg* Dostoevsky writes two short pieces, 'The Apartment,' and 'The Child,' both of which make "assaults" on the child of the landlady in whose house he and his son both lodged. Although, perhaps because, they betray everything he holds dear, including himself, the pieces are filled with artistic power. "*I have lost my place in my soul*," he thinks, having put the pen down.

The Ethics of Embodiment: Philosophy and literature

What counts is what we are, and the way we deepen our relationship with the world and with others, a relationship that can be both one of love of all that exists and of desire for its transformation. Then you put the point of the pen on the white page, work out a certain angle so that it produces the black signs which make sense, and wait to see what comes out of all this. It is also true that you often end by tearing everything up.
- Italo Calvino, in interview

People ask Elizabeth the questions that people ask everyone. Strangers ask her in bars. Family members who she hasn't seen in years ask her. The other day, her doctor asked. They ask, "So what do you do?" And after that the questions narrow. "And what is your thesis on?" And then, almost always, "Have you met Coetzee?"

As the questions continue Elizabeth is already preparing her response to the following one. On her tongue waiting are the words and the correct tone. A tone of friendly acquiescence, an informed tone. Usually she will try to add to her voice a sympathetic edge that implies: 'I'm trying to simplify this. It's ok if you've never heard of this author, or if you're realising right now that you wish you'd never asked the question, the response to which is uninteresting to you.' Usually as the questions proceed, the questioner's eyes flit downwards, or away, as they realise they have found no common ground with the answers Elizabeth is giving. Isn't this the point of questioning, after all? To find the mutual, and then to pounce!

Sometimes they say they have read *Disgrace*, but often they have nothing to say about the book beyond that.

To the last question, Elizabeth's response is always a little rambling. "So have you met Coetzee?" they ask. And she smiles, maybe laughs a little, and says "Oh no, I couldn't. He's a hero of mine, I'd be like a giggling schoolgirl." Usually they smile and groan a little and say, "Oh you should though! Surely he would be interested in reading your work, maybe even flattered!" "Oh no," Elizabeth says. "He is reclusive and very curt with journalists. He's had many books and articles written about him already." "Oh you should meet him, he's just over in Adelaide!" And at this point the conversation usually peters out as Elizabeth continues to make smiling excuses, and feels herself to be weak; feels the absence of the Story of Meeting Coetzee weigh heavily, until the questions and answers wilt to nothing.

But of course she has imagined the meeting.

Adelaide University is where Elizabeth's father took his doctorate in botany. He had an office below ground level, with just a sliver of window sticking up above the surface of the pavement. She and her mother and sister would go to visit him, crouch down at his window and wave through the glass. Her father wore a white lab coat and with his pointy black beard looked like an eccentric professor in his cave of wonder. He had a fern in his office which curled coyly if you stroked it down the middle. There was a machine you turned on with a big red switch until it growled loudly, and shook, and the little ball it held would spin in crazy patterns over a surface shiny as mercury. The walls were covered in odd pictures, newspaper clippings, notes, cartoons. Elizabeth would always stare at one picture of a big red barrel of wet cement with a pair of her father's boots sticking up-side-down out of the top. She knew it was a joke someone had played. It was set up.

Her father would smell like a foreign person. The men who came in all had beards and white coats, and the same smell, which was somehow the smell of white, a smell of science. They laughed loudly and spoke to her father in ways Elizabeth did not understand. She rec-ognised the parlance later as that between colleagues. They'd walk along the halls back outside and the people in white coats would smile down at her quizzically, sometimes patting her head or asking her a question about school. She would tighten her grip on her mother's skirt and remain silent until their faces, after a flash of sadness, bobbed out of her view, back to adult level. On a patch of green they would sit and eat the sandwiches her mother had packed, her father stretching his legs out from under his white coat. From here they could see a long squat ornately-bricked building, and it was this that Elizabeth imagined now, when she pictured the meeting with Coetzee.

What could she possibly say to the man? Surely he would, he must, tower over her, perhaps touch her head, and ask her a question about school. Surely she would reach out for the safety of her mother's skirt, and finding it absent, would let her arm drop, would be suffused with silence, until the features of Coetzee's, the stranger's, face flashed sadness or annoyance as he returned abruptly to the adult – the real – world.

*

Costello's progress, human to ape

Some questions to ask of the novel *Elizabeth Costello*, after putting it down, are: what are the links, and what is the progression, if any, be-tween the Lessons? Are there interlocking themes addressed? Does Costello go through that arc of change readers expect of their lead characters: becoming something different by the book's end? At first glance it seems Costello wakes and sleeps, jolts perhaps, in and out of each Lesson. She is momentarily reborn, just as the issues she is con-ducting lessons on need to be formulated and introduced to her audi-ence; and then, just as her lectures need concluding phrases, she too is laid down at the end of each chapter, with intimations of death re-sounding around those final full stops:

" 'It will soon be over.'" (115, end of Lesson 4);

"*Mother gone; old Mr Phillips burned to a powder and scattered to the winds; of the world we grew up in, just you and I left. Sister of my youth, do not die in a foreign field and leave me without an answer!*" (155, end of Lesson 5; original itals.);

"Something should pass between them, sudden as lightning, that will illuminate the landscape for her, even if afterwards it returns to its native darkness. But the corridor, it seems, is empty." (182, end of Lesson 6).

Does the recurring finality of the lesson-endings result in a patchiness or disjointedness of character and narrative? Some critics have argued that yes, since Coetzee wrote and published most chapters separately, there is little to substantiate a novel, little development, little that abides: "Coetzee seems simply hamstrung by the hybrid status of his inventions" (Mars-Jones 2003). But I would argue that at the heart of each lesson is a cluster of close-knit ideas centred on the notion of *embodiment* which we find entangled with authorial *imagination* and surrounding them, a proposal for *literature* as an appropriate medium to discuss matters outside the realm of *reason*. Coetzee returns to these four ideas repeatedly throughout the novel. These are loaded terms, and in the following chapter are used as they are bound to Co-etzee's contexts. In comparing 'literature' and 'philosophy' for example, I refer as much to the respective acts or *writings* of each medium as to those contested epistemological definitions which might be applied to either term. Like Costello's, this essay may strike the two elements of broad definition and specific interpretation together ambiguously – the technique aims to further the essay's own inernal argument. Here, Lessons 3, 4 and 6 emerge as prominent in addressing these four central themes, and indeed are the most forcefully memorable chapters of the book.

     Lesson 3, the first part of the double-Lesson on 'The Lives of Animals,' acts as a forerunner to the copycat irony of Lesson 8 with a short story by Franz Kafka providing Costello with a landscape for her narrative. This time it is Kafka's 'A Report to an Academy', which is an address by Red Peter, an ape trained to be human. Costello admits to feeling a little like Red Peter as she stands before a theatre of academics there to adulate her life's achievements. Although Norma, her daughter-in-law, accuses her of rambling, "She has lost her thread"

(Coetzee 2003a: 75), Costello does eventually explain the similarity. She wants to talk about animals: why it is wrong that they should suffer at the hands of human industries, and wrong, indeed, that they should be bred in order to be killed and their flesh eaten. To talk about these matters, however, to a theatre of academics, requires tact and an appropriate language, a language Costello knows is available to her: "It is the language of Aristotle and Porphyry, of Augustine and Aquinas, of Descartes and Bentham, of, in our day, Mary Midgley and Tom Regan. It is a philosophical language in which we can discuss and debate what kind of souls animals have, whether they reason…whether they have rights in respect to us" (66). Indeed, when Peter Singer responded to this lecture as delivered by Coetzee at Princeton University in 1998, it was the response of a philosopher using philosophical language. Even when Singer attempts a fictional dialogue with his daughter Naomi, as an element of his reply, the 'conversation' is quickly exposed as the means towards the well-reasoned end:

> Naomi: I can see what she's getting at. When you kill a bat, you take away everything that the bat has, its entire existence. Killing a human being can't do more than that.
> Peter: Yes, it can…The value that is lost when something is emptied depends on what was there when it was full, and there is more to human existence than there is to bat existence. (Singer 1999: 90)

Singer illustrates his point using an analogy of two liquids being poured down the sink, first a carton of soymilk, then a bottle of Kahlúa liqueur, to demonstrate that, when spilt, one has more value (at least to his daughter) than the other. "The value that is lost when something is emptied depends on what was there when it was full," he says.

As discussed with regard to Elizabeth Chandos's postscript, there is often a distinction made between analogy and metaphor, the one seeking to clarify, the other paving the way for subversion, the poetic, or 'analytic symbolism' as Lacan had it. The attempted abstraction of the two glasses as an illustrative analogy seems counterproductive here in a discussion about fiction and embodiment. Costello offers, as an alternative to the indirect abstraction of analogy – *it is like, what if I was holding, it is comparable to* – the direct verb *is*, the language of metaphor. She also suggests that the two – analogy and metaphor – are not so remote from each other as their apparently opposite descriptive purposes might suggest. In fact, she moves between the two phrases "it is *like*" and "it *is*" with fluency: "For instants at a time…I know what it is like to be a corpse… For a moment we *are* that knowledge. We live the impossible: we live beyond death." Later she continues, "Do I know what it is like for me to be a corpse or do I know what it is like for a corpse to be a corpse? The distinction seems to me trivial…For an instant…I am alive inside that contradiction, dead and alive at the same time" (Coetzee 2003a: 76-7). Here Costello's call for literature as an alternative to philosophy and reason is evident through her conflation of analogy and metaphor: she suggests that the subversion and 'making poetic' of metaphor is, in fact, the way to clarification. Where science and philosophy *use* analogy – as Singer used the two glasses – as a tool towards clarification, Costello posits analogy and metaphor – linguistic figures of speech – as the actual sites of clarification.

Singer does not enter his own analogy, does not, as Costello does with her corpse-self, *become* that knowledge. The same can be said of Singer's attempt at creating a fictional dialogue between two characters – he does not enter his fiction; we finish the discourse with no insight into the characters of Peter and Naomi, no awareness of their setting, position, relationship. Quite simply, we do not believe that they are *people*, in a fictional sense. Like the character of Norma, who has "very proper doubts" about Costello's lectures, and who voices "all the obvious objections" (Singer 1999: 91), Singer's 'characters' are mouthpieces for reasonable arguments. The intriguing aspect of Elizabeth Costello, the thing, perhaps, that has made her so difficult to get rid of – or 'take care of' in the language of *Slow Man* – is the fact that she is not defined by her arguments, instead the arguments are defined by her. She somehow clambers out of realism to enter the real, and this is the central development which ties each lesson to the next.

Singer's dialogue is just the kind of language Costello wants to resist in her discussion of animals. Just as Red Peter the ape was taught to reason as a human reasons, taught that reason was the very function that separates ape from human, Costello feels she too, simply by the weight of human history, is forced to accept reason is, as she puts it, "the being of the universe". Whereas it is her contention, and deep feeling, that reason is a much more specific occurrence: "Reason is the being of a certain spectrum of human thinking" (Coetzee 2003a: 67). In Kafka's 'A Report to an Academy' Red Peter speaks of finding it difficult to remember his life as an ape, speaks of his memory closing behind him like a door: "I could have returned at first, had human beings allowed it, through an archway as wide as the span of heaven over the earth, but as I spurred myself into my forced career, the opening narrowed and shrank behind me" (Kafka 1958: 147). It is an apt metaphor for what Costello is also saying about the options of human thinking. She contends that when philosophers like Nagel argue we can never know "what it is like for a *bat* to be a bat" (Nagel 1974: 439), we are simply restricting ourselves, allowing that wide archway of possibility to close behind us until all we have is one narrow passageway: reason. Costello offers the alternative: embodiment. "To thinking, cogitation, I oppose fullness, embodiedness, the sensation of being…This fullness contrasts starkly with Descartes' key state, [*cogito, ergo sum*] which has an empty feel to it: the feel of a pea rattling around in a shell" (Coetzee 2003a: 78). The difference between writers and philosophers has been observed earlier in Lesson 1, Costello's son watching as his mother goes through the motions of another radio interview: "A writer, not a thinker. Writers and thinkers: chalk and cheese. No, not chalk and cheese: fish and fowl. But which is she, the fish or the fowl? Which is her medium: water or air?" (10). These last two questions, which may seem strangely irrelevant to the evidently clear-cut simile, draw attention again to the particular undertaking of the writer: to enter metaphor, not as symbol, but as embodied nature; the water and the air not as abstractions, but wet or windy reality.

Throughout Lesson 4, Costello reiterates the contrast, this time using poems by Rilke and Ted Hughes to expound upon the difference between writing an animal as a symbol, and writing an animal, as Costello says Hughes does, "feeling his way towards a different kind of being-in-the-world" (95). It is, however, when the reader reaches Lesson 6 that Costello's argument for embodiment encounters a question which challenges the straightforward dualism it has remained confined to so far. The question: is it ever morally wrong to push or press oneself into imagining the being of another?

The Dark Chamber: Ethics and ambiguity

In the 2006 film *Capote* which dramatises Truman Capote researching and writing his "non-fiction masterpiece" *In Cold Blood*, the filmmakers also present, with deliberation, the moral dilemma of the author. The film cuts from scenes in which Capote interviews a murderer with a lover's tender concern, to scenes of his New York literary triumph and festivities in high society. This sort of juxtaposition also concerns Elizabeth Costello, and echoes back through Coetzee's books, particularly to the figure of Dostoevsky in *Master of Petersburg*: the author thrives on pain, the author may even go so far as to manipulate the true pain of others in order to create his best work. In the film it is implied that Perry Smith not only murdered his victims in cold blood, but that Capote also wrote, and maybe shortened a life, in cold blood; perhaps that the filmmakers themselves threaded the reels cold-bloodedly. When Smith is hanged Capote, we assume, cannot help but wonder if he hastened the end of this life in order to find an end for his novel.

A scene of hanging is also at the centre of Paul West's book *The Very Rich Hours of Count von Stauffenberg*, the book that Elizabeth Costello has just finished reading when we find her in Lesson 6. Costello is deeply disturbed by the book: she feels it to be 'sick,' 'depraved,' 'obscene,' and finally lands upon "the sturdy Calvinist word *evil*" (Coetzee 2003a: 157–9), to describe the text, particularly the scenes she relates involving the execution of Hitler's would-be assassins. Before she arrives at these chapters, she reflects, "all was going well enough," implying that it was only those few horrifying scenes that affected her judgement of the book as a whole. In fact if one reads West's book one finds the scenes of horror to be brief in comparison with the bulk of the text which is a minutely-crafted portrayal of an historical event: the individuals, episodes and social implications. The *weight* of those scenes of horror, then, relative to the book as a whole, is enormous. For Costello, the plot, narrative and general course of the book are overshadowed by the *evil* in those short scenes: she cannot think of the book as a book anymore, but as the scene of a violence done to her.

This strange relative weight will be discussed in greater detail presently. For now, I will explore some of the ethical predicaments, or at least questions, that Coetzee's Lesson 6 presents. This is the place in the novel when the cluster of linked themes – embodiment, imagination, literature and reason – reaches a point of crisis and is pushed forward, indicating Costello's progression as a character. There is first of all the question of whether literature, and art in general, should necessarily come under moral scrutiny, or whether, as Costello used to believe in her former, more liberal paper, that "the civilization of the West is based on belief in unlimited and illimitable endeavour, it is too late for us to do anything about that" (160). Should there, in fact, be limits upon what is presented artistically, she now wonders, and should the worth of art be judged on its ethics? In his 1998 essay 'The Ethical Criticism of Art,' which appears in two major anthologies on the philosophy of literature, Berys Gaut introduces the term *ethicism* as "the thesis that the ethical assessment of attitudes manifested by works of art is a legitimate aspect of the aesthetic evaluation of those works" (Gaut 2004: 355). In clarifying his definition Gaut keeps ethicism and censorship distinct: "All that follows from ethicism is that if a work manifests morally bad attitudes it is to that extent aesthetically flawed, flawed as a work of art. The fact that a work of art is aesthetically flawed is not grounds for its censorship" (356). Although in Lesson 6 Costello is not so much concerned with an author's obscured particular moral attitudes, but more with a kind of general meta-ethics, Gaut's expression is worth exploring for the light it might throw on the issues tackled throughout *Elizabeth Costello*.

Ethical assessments of art can be found in almost all modern reviews, their task being, unlike literary criticism, to provide a judgement of a work for a wide audience. These ethical appraisals can be as simple as a particular word-choice. The word 'important,' for instance, which is used frequently by reviewers to describe a film, book, artwork or musical work which addresses some defining historical event, places the work on an ethical level and inevitably indicates the reviewer's assessment of it. Even if they are not entirely impressed with the artistry of the work, the reviewers are influenced in their evaluation by the significance of its ethical stance. Sometimes reviewers are torn between the work's ethical and artistic merits, and in the end their assessment reflects their attitude to each. A number of Coetzee's novels have received a similar mixed response, most notably *Waiting for the Barbarians* and *Disgrace*, the former being undoubtedly Coetzee's most graphically violent and perhaps darkest work, the one that first drew him worldwide attention, in fact. The books each received numerous awards, but were met by reviewers with wariness.

All recognised the books' artistic merits, the haunting nature of their allegories, their disconcerting central male figures, their stylistic beauty. What made reviewers uneasy was the dislocation of the texts. What some were not sure of, it seems, was, 'Is he, or is he not, making a point about the current state of South Africa? And if he is, then why veil the point; why the metaphor?' As Schott wrote of *Barbarians*: "It moves tentatively and conditionally, and most often in the direction of irony and ambiguity" (Schott 1982: 2). And even more damning, Peter Lewis from *Times Literary Supplement* in 1980, "This kind of fiction as a whole, peopled as it is mainly by stereotypes, is often in danger of moving so far away from the familiar in its determination to establish universals that it defeats its own purpose" (Lewis 1980: 1271). Is the recognisably ethical and political nature of the novels what, in fact, establishes them as 'important,' or 'good'? And are these reviewers accusing Coetzee of a coy avoidance of his ethical responsibilities to the specificity of immorality?

To place this discussion in a further context, the idea of *embodiment* must be more broadly introduced. In a 1986 essay entitled 'Into the Dark Chamber,' Coetzee wrote about his book *Waiting for the Barbarians* in relation to its themes of torture. He writes plainly, perhaps riskily so, about Vorster Square, the Headquarters of the Johannesburg security police:

> Let us be clear about the situation of the prisoner who falls under suspicion of a crime against the state. What happens in Vorster Square is nominally illegal... What the prisoner knows, what the police know he knows, is that he is helpless against whatever they choose to do to him. The torture room thus becomes like the bed-chamber of the pornographer's fantasy where, insulated from moral or physical restraint, one human being is free to exercise his imagination to the limits in the performance of vileness upon the body of another. (Coetzee 1986b: 13)

The phrase that leaps at once from the page, if one is alert to the simile being evinced, is "free to exercise his imagination to the limits." Such a positive phrase, one used, probably, in many art, film, music and creative writing classes, 'Feel free to exercise your imagination here.' It is no mistake that Coetzee uses it here to describe the torturer and his dark chamber. This is the very place, in fact, where the novelist finds inspiration, simply because of its inaccessibility. Coetzee quotes John T. Irwin on the character of the novelist: "It is precisely because

[he] stands outside the dark door, wanting to enter the dark room but unable to, that he is a novelist, that he must imagine what takes place beyond the door. Indeed, it is just that tension toward the dark room that he cannot enter that makes that room the source of all his imaginings – the womb of art" (Coetzee 1986b: 13).[8] Again it is the idea of inaccessibility, the *inhuman*, just like Nagel's pronouncement of the inaccessibility of the life of a bat, that sparks the author's creative curiosity, and her desire for embodiment. But the difference between trying to embody a bat, a tiger, an ape, as distinct from a torturer or a hangman, is, in the end, an ethical one.

   This is, I argue, where the progression of *Elizabeth Costello*'s themes comes into play: the lessons are not only linked by a cluster of correlated ideas – embodiment, imagination, literature and reason – they are moving toward something, and here the shift from Lessons 3 and 4 to Lesson 6 is a progression from asking how? and whether? to asking why? and why not? Costello's impassioned argument for embodiment and literature over reason and philosophy becomes embroiled, in Lesson 6, in the question of moral limitation. At the same time as Costello is enunciating this progression, the reader is aware of the same questions with relation to Coetzee's 'embodiment' of his subject, Costello. The reader may perhaps begin by asking *how* Costello and Coetzee are similar, whether they are, in fact, two parts of the same whole; later, though, they may ask, as Paul West does in his review of Lesson 6 in *Harper's Magazine*, *why* Coetzee chooses this woman as his subject, a woman with whom he has so much in common, but whose views on ethics, as West sees it, are the ironic opposite of Coetzee's own:

> I found myself drawn sotto voce into the discreet spectacle of an author banishing a cantankerous ghost whose primal views he did not share but had nonetheless haunted him... Do the hints get through, then, enough to convince us he's on the side of West rather than Costello? I think so. Costello herself is made to claim that West will have "defenders by the thousand," dubbing him "not a devil but a hero." (West 2004: 89)

West is in a position unlike any other reader of the novel, in finding himself a (silent) character, and his book a catalyst towards Costello's

---

[8] Coetzee cites John T. Irwin's 'Doubling and Incest/Repetition and Revenge: A Speculative Reading of Faulkner' in this passage.

most controversial lecture in which she cautions bluntly: "I do not believe it will be good for you or for me to hear [from the 'terrible pages' of the book]… I do not believe it was good for Mr West…to write those pages" (Coetzee 2003a: 173). His picture, then, of Coetzee banishing a disagreeable ghost and dropping clues towards his actual support of West, comes from a unique readerly stance, and is indeed unique amongst appraisals of the Coetzee-Costello relationship. Most reviewers assume, with Peter Singer, that Costello is a kind of fictional alter-ego for Coetzee, a relationship which carries with it enough ambiguity to make Costello's contentious views beyond reproach.

Why, the obvious question emerges, as we progress from observing the relationship to interrogating it, would an author embody himself in fiction? Isn't the high aim of writing a literary character to withdraw from the self in order to inhabit another? In fact, aren't authors known for becoming rather tetchy if it is suggested they resemble their main characters? In the same article, West speaks affectionately of 'Stauff,' an historical figure West has fictionalised and now interacts with, hears speaking, after his death: "Lines, not mine, that fit Stauff (as I call him), if you are any sort of literary person, include 'Unspeakable ... is the sorrow you bid me renew,' from the opening lines of The Aeneid's second book" (West 2004: 92). In other words there is a sense in which Stauff is independent, and may protest his indecorous un-burial. As I discussed in 'Where is Coetzee?' the strange symbiosis between author and character is often one of mutual creation, but slips, as images do, from the peaceful still of two hands drawing each other, to the chaotic master-slave relationship of Sinbad and the old man. It is my contention that there is no easy line to be drawn from Coetzee to Costello, and no easy division either. Since the book is above all, in my view, a study of the writer, the writer's life and processes, then surely part of that process is to experience what it is like to both embody a character and to emerge from that embodiment. The strange dipping from one state to another, one being to another, is at the heart of both *Elizabeth Costello* and *Slow Man*.

The point that seems to be missed by those who would criticise *Barbarians* for its ambiguity or universality in relation to the contemporary issue of tyranny, is that the character of the magistrate is defined not only by his position in the frontier-town, but by his position in the novel – that of narrator. The magistrate is an author figure – he too battles with the dark door:

> I know somewhat too much; and from this knowledge, once one
> has been infected, there seems to be no recovering. I ought never
> to have taken my lantern to see what was going on in the hut by
> the granary. On the other hand, there was no way, once I had
> picked up the lantern, for me to put it down again. The knot loops
> in upon itself; I cannot find an end. (Coetzee 1980: 21)

As such he is also, like Coetzee, engaged in this strange cyclic immersion and emergence, both entering and observing the characters and events around him. To be anything other than ambiguous would be to misrepresent the position of the divided author, as Coetzee sees it. Just like Coetzee's other protagonist author-figures – Dostoevsky, Mrs Curren, Susan Barton – the magistrate is both the mouthpiece for allegorical summary, and a particular being with a body upon which detailed tortures may be enacted: "its head is gripped and a pipe is pushed down its gullet and pints of salt water are poured into it till it coughs and retches and flails and voids itself" (115). Perhaps Coetzee himself recognises his books' potential to be criticised for their evasion of a rigid ethical stance, although evasion is perhaps not the right word for a sincere representation of the position of the author. It is the desperation that the books' own ambiguity engenders, as seen so clearly in Lady Chandos's tortured struggle with metaphor, which makes them so compelling, and so undeniably valid.

Two Suspended Elements: sentence, narrative, text

To return, then, to the question of the ethics of embodiment, West's review suggests further interesting enquiries, dismayed as he is by Costello's conservative move towards censorship. He ends his article in defence of art's purpose to reflect reality, whatever that is:

> We have all only just scraped the surface of what might seem a
> horrendous problem: starting out to denounce horror, yet, in the
> end, accepting it for its own sake, because it further reveals the
> unique license of human creative power. No matter how gross the
> outcome, it will be better to paddle around in its dark miasma than
> to ban it. So long as men are vile, so can art be too, and maybe
> even after. (West 2004: 94)

In terms of the vileness of humanity, it is difficult to go past the events of the Holocaust. The wealth of literature on the ethics of writing the Holocaust is testament to the paradox at the heart of, as Blanchot puts it, 'writing the disaster': "The disaster, unexperienced. It is what es-capes the very possibility of experience – it is the limit of writing. This must be repeated: the disaster de-scribes" (Blanchot 1986: 7). Undoubtedly the most uncomfortable moments of *Elizabeth Costello* are those in which Costello compares, repeatedly compares, the Holo-caust with the modern mass slaughtering of animals. She does it not only in her lectures – always excusing herself afterwards with an apology, "That is the last cheap point I will be scoring" (Coetzee 2003a: 66) – but also privately, in confession to her son on finding "fragments of corpses," packages of meat, in everyday places in peo-ple's homes:

> It is as if I were to visit friends, and to make some polite remark about the lamp in their living room, and they were to say, 'Yes, it's nice isn't it? Polish-Jewish skin it's made of, we find that's best, the skins of young Polish-Jewish virgins. (Coetzee 2003a: 115)

One voice, the letter of Abraham Stern, a respected poet, reacts in pro-test to Costello's presumption: "If Jews were treated like cattle, it does not follow that cattle are treated like Jews. The inversion insults the memory of the dead" (94). Aside from the particular offence Costello seems to be causing by equating racism with speciesism, the more general question of using the Holocaust as an example, as a metaphor – using it artistically as it were – is still highly contentious.

In his essay 'I Was Not There', historian Raul Hilberg traces the removes from compilation involved in historical writing and the im-plicated risks of license:

> The step beyond compilation is reportage...How much more re-moved from the actuality of reportage are those works whose au-thors have introduced a theory or theme?... They may be shrewd, insightful, or masterful, but they take a larger risk, and all the more so, if they take a poetic license to subtract something from the crude reality for the sake of heightened effect. (Hilberg in Lang 1988: 22-3)

If it is problematic to attempt a fictional embodiment of someone liv-ing during the Holocaust because of affected drama, how much more problematic is Costello's further remove from 'crude reality' to the point of analogy? In February 2007, four years after the publication of *Elizabeth Costello*, Coetzee put his own name to the argument that the mass slaughter, or 'processing' of human beings during the Holocaust of the Second World War was just like, and was in fact instigated by, the methods of the industrial stockyard – methods and processes which continue on a massive scale today. He rests the crux of his argument on these paragraphs:

> The transformation of animals into production units dates back to the late 19th century, and since that time we have already had one warning on the grandest scale that there is something deeply, cosmically wrong with regarding and treating fellow beings as mere units of any kind. This warning came so loud and clear that one would have thought it impossible to ignore. It came when, in the 20th century, a group of powerful and bloody-minded men in Germany hit on the idea of adapting the methods of the industrial stockyard, as pioneered and perfected in Chicago, to the slaughter – or what they preferred to call the processing – of human beings.
>
> Of course we cried out in horror when we found out what they had been up to. What a terrible crime to treat human beings like cattle – if we had only known beforehand. But our cry should more accurately have been: what a terrible crime to treat human beings like units in an industrial process. And that cry should have had a postscript: what a terrible crime – come to think of it, a crime against nature – to treat any living being like a unit in an industrial process. (Coetzee 2007d: 17)

Coetzee is attempting to widen our view of crime and horror: he takes an event which is already accepted historically, by the masses, to be a terrible corruption, a black mark against the human race, and directly compares it with an event which is yet to be seen by the masses in the same way. Coetzee is claiming that the two are equivalent. He is not *using* the Holocaust as an abstract means towards clarification, but rather finds the site of clarification to be the figure of speech itself – the two elements in suspense with one another, equalling and entering each other. Once again, Elizabeth Chandos and the turmoil of her frustration with metaphor, that looping agonised voice, is asserting itself, as good postscripts do, into a rereading of the text: "It is like a contagion, saying one thing always for another" (Coetzee 2003a: 228). The problem of metaphor addresses itself here to the problem of embodiment. Costello struggles to speak of the mass slaughter of animals, an issue which bewilders her, stuns her; she can only find the means towards it through removal. Above, Hilberg views with wariness the synthesis of crude documents into narratives, the stringing together of sentences using only raw statistics; yet sometimes clarity arrives through removal and distance, or better, a thing is seen only by contrast with another. The same principle of language is at work in the idea of embodiment, and indeed with the idea of writing at all.

In fact, the voice of Lady Chandos seems to act as one final dissenting call from Costello's audience, asking, as it does, for relief from the endless cycles of words that never arrive at meaning. In a way, Lady Chandos is echoing the arguments of the philosophers, albeit in tones far removed from the measured sentences of Singer and Nagel. At the very beginning of his article 'What is it like to be a bat?' Nagel criticises the way many reductionist philosophers use analogies from modern science to expound their particular view of the mind-body problem. He writes:

> It is most unlikely that any of these unrelated examples of successful reduction will shed light on the relation of the mind to the brain. But philosophers share the general human weakness for explanations of what is incomprehensible in terms suited for what is familiar and well understood, though entirely different. (Nagel 1974: 435)

This is the 'human weakness' Lady Chandos also baulks at, as she rejects, one after the other, her 'wayfarer,' her 'flaming swords,' her 'dog in the sun,' as diversions from the unutterable heart of her trouble. Yet Costello argues, and, I believe, Coetzee argues, that this is not a weakness at all, but a strength, the strength of literature and its power beyond philosophy. It is not the mind, reason, experience, or consciousness that open the passageway from one being to another, but that most flimsy and unfashionable of words, the heart: "The heart is the seat of a faculty, *sympathy*, that allows us to share at times the being of another. Sympathy has everything to do with the subject and little to do with the object" (Coetzee 2003: 79). Marion Bloom never existed, as Costello points out, but was brought to life, given an existence first by James Joyce and followed by Costello herself, who also never existed, but was brought to life by Coetzee. If sympathy and embodiment have "everything to do with the subject," then Costello is positioned as both sympathetic imaginer of another, and revelatory signpost to her creator, Coetzee.

The two, author and character, are held in a suspended state, each engaged in the task of embodying another, each therefore designing a looping space from which to embody themselves. The self-same tension exists between the two elements of a metaphor and analogy – the contrasting space between the two complicates, subverts and enriches the apprehension of each. The purpose, in each case, both literary embodiment and linguistic expression, is far removed from Nagel's, and philosophy's, of reduction, of 'shedding light on,' of 'explanations'. The purpose of these suspended distances is, in the end, the purpose of literature itself, the purpose of placing the pen to the page in that primal act of separation and metaphor: to create and imagine otherness, to renew and subvert perspective, to see things again, through the faculty of sympathy.

This observation on the purpose of distance can be taken one step further. In an article on the task of the imagination in *Disgrace*, Mike Marais charts the course of David Lurie's awakening as a sympathetic being, identifying Lurie's empathy for the lame dogs as: "the logic of *ek-stasis* and self-sacrifice that informs Coetzee's conception of the imagination…To sympathize, Lurie must lose, indeed sacrifice or offer, himself" (Marais 2006: 78). Once again, the idea of sacrifice has its precursors in Coetzee's other works, including *Master of Petersburg* in which Dostoevsky is granted an interview with Maximov, the chief of police in charge of the inquiry into Dostoevsky's stepson's death. The great author discusses reading: "'Reading is being the arm, being the axe *and* being the skull; reading is giving yourself up, not holding yourself at a distance and jeering.'" To which Maximov replies "'You speak of reading as though it is demon-possession,'" and dismisses Dostoevsky as being "feverish" (Coetzee 1994: 47). Perhaps the differences between reading and writing have been collapsed since Barthes' 'The Death of the Author,' in which the commonality of language transcends those boundaries: "Language knows a 'subject,' not a 'person,' and this subject, empty outside of the very enunciation which defines it, suffices to make language 'hold together,' suffices, that is to say, to exhaust it" (Barthes 1977: 145). Accordingly, the writer becomes another reader, entering again through language the being of the axe-wielder, the being of the axed. Blanchot, however, had a slightly different perspective on the matter of reading and writing. He writes in his 'From Dread to Language,': "If I read, language…makes me adhere to a common meaning which, because it is not directly connected to what I am, interposes itself between my dread and me. But if I write, I am the one who is making the common meaning adhere to language" (Blanchot 1999: 358). It is a subtle difference, but one which addresses again the moment of writing, and the transferral of that moment to page, and to reader.

As Marais continues, and as the unstable characters of David Lurie and Elizabeth Costello reiterate, the ideal logic of *ek-stasis* is more motioned towards than enacted in the text. In the end, "[the imagination] is located in the self and will thus always, to a lesser or greater extent, be limited by the desires and antipathies of the self of which it is ultimately an emanation or expression" (Marais 2006: 80). Thus, as Marais concludes, the meditation on the imagination in *Disgrace* argues for the inevitable excess, incompletion and destruction of that which it seeks to imagine. This then transfers to the novel's reading:

> The novel seeks to ensure that its own reading repeats the unrepeatable encounter with alterity of which it can only ever bear a trace. If this were to transpire, the reader would gain a sense of, and so be inspired by, that which exceeds the grasp of the imagination, and which...turns his or her reading into an "orphic commemoration," a *katabatic* work of mourning. (Marais 2006: 88-9)

Coetzee's Elizabeth Costello texts do not only meditate again upon this idea of reading as a work of mourning, a search for the trace of an "unrepeatable encounter with alterity," but also *enter* this idea, and explore it openly. Thus they again become examples of Derrida's fictive narrativity: "fiction *of* narration as well as fiction as narration: fictive narration as the simulacrum of narration and not only as the narration of an imaginary history" (Derrida 1992: 199). As Coetzee writes in a short essay, 'Fictional Beings,' this is a paradoxical situation for the writer:

> Storytellers (a) inhabit real beings and represent them from the inside, and also (b) by this process create them out of nothing and turn them into real beings. It is a paradoxical position, but it does appear to be a position of some importance to human societies, which, in a paradoxical movement of their own, both (a) entertain it, and (b) dismiss it as nonsense. (Coetzee 2003b: 134)

Just as the novels both inhabit and observe their own narration, so too are their characters both inhabited – embodied – and observed, using the creative distance of metaphor.

The same principle is thus at work at every level of the fiction. At the level of the sentence we find the distance between two elements of a metaphor. At the level of the narrative, we find embodiment, the author in suspense with her character. And at the level of text, we encounter the same principle of distance: the work itself in suspense between its narrative and its own narration.

These observations about the positioning of two suspended elements at every level of the fiction carries with it further weight than mere structural arrangement. As two great ethical philosophers, Sartre and Levinas, have observed, the suspended distance between one and another is the basic condition for ethical responsibility, ethical response and ethical action. Sartre said in an interview from 1980, the year of his death:

> [By] ethics I mean that every consciousness…has a dimension…the dimension of obligation… By obligation I mean that at every moment that I am conscious of anything or do anything, there exists a kind of requisition… [that] results in the fact that the action I want to perform includes a kind of inner constraint…Everything that takes place for a consciousness at any given moment is necessarily linked to, and often is even engendered by, the presence of another. (Sartre and Lévy 87)

Levinas used the image of the self facing another to discuss this same suspended state. As one commentator put it: "the self's responsibility to the other who faces is immediate, originary, and irreducible" (Robbins 1991: 1052). The moment of divide, then, when an author puts pen to paper, and when she attempts to make that leap towards embodying another, is fraught with questions of responsibility, obligation and constraint. As discussed earlier, the divides prompted by the moment of writing are multiple and varied, and each involves this same ethical positioning, one facing another: author faces reader, faces character, faces their own self-division. Authors are perhaps constantly weighing the equation in their minds: is art worth this betrayal? Is this beauty? and if it is, then what is beauty's value? Is beauty's value worth someone's life, is it worth their soul, is it worth their trust? In the Elizabeth Costello short story 'As A Woman Grows Older,' published the year after the novel *Elizabeth Costello* was released, Costello mulls viscerally over the question of beauty with her art-dealer daughter:

> Is beauty not just another consumable, like wine? One drinks it down, it gives one a brief, pleasing, heady feeling, but what does it leave behind? The residue of wine is, excuse the word, piss; what is the residue of beauty? What is the good of it? Does beauty make us better people? (Coetzee 2004)

This is the ethical question residing behind artistic creation. When an author puts pen to page and comes face-to-face with another being, who holds her in suspense with herself, these questions about the weight and the worth of beauty, the weight of horror and 'evil', are always hovering around her pen. Can a horrific occurrence justify its own retelling, its transferral, its *spread*, because it lends itself to the beauty of form? Is beauty, is art, worth the ransacking of the last minutes of the old men, those would-be assassins of Hitler – a question West himself inquires after with his inclusion of a film-camera during the scenes of hanging:

> The camera missed none of this, although it could not smell the soiled pants from the last wearers, or what began pooling under him as he twisted, unable even to gasp. Face dark as liver. Froth. Penis like the iron crotch struts that jutted out, with metal foreskin flared from the burning stakes of the Inquisition...Unspeakable and unwatchable, the film of that evening's events, all the way from the pitiful eight squatting in shackles in their cells to the last agonized twist, went to S'gruber that very night for him to drool over. (West 1989: 298-9)

Unspeakable and unwatchable indeed, yet here is West speaking it, and here we are watching it. Does it do us, or the author, any good? It is, perhaps, the wrong question, but in asking it Costello reveals herself to us, embodied, at times 'like' a real person and at times, a real person.

The metaphor of the real

Coetzee calls the worth of the beauty of art into question again in his essay on the 1961 film *The Misfits*, which was based on an original screenplay by Arthur Miller. Much of the review is the kind of deft, terse textual analysis one expects from reading Coetzee's essays: he examines the term 'misfit' both as it appears in the world of the film – cowboys in Eisenhower's America – and off-camera in the tragic 'forlorn' figure of Marilyn Monroe. There comes a point in the essay, however, when it is almost as though another voice has stepped in to look at the film from a different angle. Coetzee notes the absence, during the credit sequence, of modern assurances that no hardship was caused to animals during the film's production. He writes, "The exhaustion and pain and terror one sees on the screen are real exhaustion and pain and terror. The horses are not acting. The horses are the real thing, being exploited by Huston…for actually being what they seem to be" (Coetzee 2007b: 225). The final line of the essay asks the question: "Who would dare to say it is just a story?" He is asking the question on behalf of the wild horses, for whom the story, screenplay, and symbolism of the film mean nothing as they, in a real historical event, run from and are eventually subjugated by, real ropes and whips.

Coetzee makes a distinction in the essay between books and film, the former, he says, working via intermediary symbols with "the idea of a hand," rather than "the visual record…of a real hand." He writes, "There is something irreducibly different about the photographic image, namely that it bears in or with itself the trace of a real historical past" (Coetzee 2007b: 226). At this point, the reader may recall Paul Rayment, sitting one-legged in his flat, looking at his treasured collection of Fauchery photographs, mulling over why he trusts the picture more than the word: "Once [pictures] leave the darkroom, they are fixed, immutable. Whereas stories – the story of the needle in the bloodstream, for instance, or the story of how he and Wayne Blight came to meet on Magill Road – seem to change shape all the time" (Coetzee 2005: 64). Later, however, Rayment discovers one of his photographs has been replaced with a copy: "It is the desecration that he feels most of all: the dead men made fun of by a couple of cocky, irreverent youths. Presumably they did it using some kind of digital technique. He could never have achieved so convincing a montage in an old-fashioned darkroom" (Coetzee 2005: 218). Not so fixed and immutable, then, are Rayment's photographic images and, I would argue, neither is the difference between books and film, both of which hold within them the distressed inscription of their making. Coetzee's question, "Who would dare say it is just a story?" can be applied to any form of storytelling: filmed, written, painted, sung, or simply told, as one person tells the story of their day to another. In every case, the distinction between what is real and what is "just a story" becomes tenuous. It is my contention that upon finishing *Eliza-*

beth Costello, one may apply Coetzee's conflation of the phrases *it is like* and *it is*, to both Costello herself, who is *like* a human being and *is* a human being, and to the even wider subject of fiction itself, which is both *like* reality and *is* reality.

We are both rational and irrational beings. Just as Coetzee both embodies and emerges from the embodiment of his character Costello, we also slip in and out of different states of being, now distancing ourselves in order to make reasonable comparisons, and now entering, embodying, another state, occupying its fullness of being. Who dare say, *it is just a story*, when at any moment an idea may shift from one 'spectrum of human thinking,' reason, to another, embodiment. This is the way the idea of the ethics of embodiment changes and progresses throughout the novel. As the distinction between realism and the real becomes tenuous, so do the lines of ethical responsibility. We arrive at the final Lesson, in which Costello, a fictional character, finds herself immersed in an overtly fictional world, but must still interact with this world, and answer to this world just as a real person in the real world might. We reread it, with the idea of embodiment lingering in our minds and discover: our imagined selves are also answering to an imagined world; it is unreasonable, it is just as real.

*

For a long time Elizabeth has felt, ever since her fervent Christian upbringing led her flat into the walls of Jericho, that there is some core to her being that has disappeared, and left her floating in mid air. She realises, one day, that all around her people are doing good. Friends are protesting at faraway detention centres, they are donating, they give away money to the homeless who ask them, they have stopped eating meat, they volunteer on the weekends, they demonstrate against injustice, they offer kindness and friendship to whomever they meet. One person particularly impresses upon her this *goodness* and leaves her feeling privileged, jealous, smaller. She has thought before about the age she lives in, with *tolerance* a new kind of religion. But she recognises now, without the film of sarcasm coating her words, it is true, at least for many members of her generation, in the circles she moves. And she decides she wants to be *better*. She happens, at the same time, to be reading an anthology edited by one of the more famous moralists of the day, Peter Singer, called *The Moral of the Story: An Anthology of Ethics through Literature*. The book, at over 600 large thin pages, is not meant to be read from end to end, but is more like a textbook, even offering helpful discussion points on each excerpt at the back. But Elizabeth reads it the wrong way, which is the right way, from beginning to end. It takes her three weeks. Afterwards, with a list of titles she wants to look up, she wanders around the second-hand bookshops feeling as though she must be glowing, like people say pregnant women glow. And she feels pregnant: justified, and irrevocably changed.

She hears that Peter Singer is coming her way, and the glowing fibres of her missing core begin, once again, to knit themselves together. *It must be happening all at once for a reason*, she thinks, unreasonably. A friend accompanies her to the lecture, one of her *good* friends, and while they are milling with the surprisingly large crowd waiting to get in, Peter Singer himself brushes past them, his arm touching hers for an instant. She recognises the man, small and gnomish, from documentaries and interviews she's seen. Once Singer is inside (she wonders why there is no secret back entrance for the presenter) the doors are opened and the crowd floods in. Elizabeth and her friend find themselves with nowhere to go once they are inside the door; all the seats are taken and people are sitting cross-legged in the aisles and at the front of the auditorium. They sit down where they are, in uncomfortably small spaces, and clutch their knees. Elizabeth has no pen, but there's no room to write anyway.

During the first half of the lecture, she is distracted by the constant knocks at the door, people trying to get in. A security man, like a Bethlehem innkeeper, opens the door, tells them there is no room. In the end, he simply stands at the door where there is a perspex window at eye level, and shakes his head sternly at the knockers. One girl defies him, opens the door, pushes deftly through and sits before he has time to stop her. 'Excuse me, excuse me, I have to be here,' Elizabeth hears her say. She has the voice of a devotee, and looks, as some people look, like a vegan. The lecture itself is not delivered very engagingly; Singer's voice is flat and annoyingly well-cadenced, a voice with a twinge of self-righteous clag at the back of the throat. There are also slides: pig farms in Texas where waste is dumped into nearby bodies of water; chicken farms where a mass of plumped and beakless birds spend their days taking one step and then the same step backwards because there is no other room; cattle farms where calves are locked in calf-sized pens and fed until they are fleshy enough to die. The same thought Elizabeth has been thinking for months now re-enters her mind with a new force: the only reason I still eat meat is because I have never seen the inside of a slaughterhouse.

So the thing happens. After a couple of weeks, she tells her family, calls them formally with her 'news,' feeling slightly silly since her sister called with 'news,' earlier in the week, and Elizabeth's own news can hardly compare. But she calls them and finds herself giving speeches with hard edges and dramatic pauses, using sentences that aren't formed in the way normal chatty sentences are formed.

She and her partner have long breathless discussions on the topic as they walk around the hilly neighbourhood, pointing cats out to each other as they dart away from their footsteps. At first Elizabeth is convinced that eating the meat of free-range animals would be accept-able, since they have experienced life's quality, the sun, have wan-dered freely, have not been pumped full of steroids and vitamins, have been killed humanely, have been given the chance to be the animal they were meant to be. Her partner disagrees. He says it is even cruel-ler to kill an animal after it has known the pleasures of life – to cut short, as it were, its natural existence, to shock it, to be unfair. 'Just as it was getting comfortable!' he says, 'It must die to service *our* pleas-ure.' She takes his point. They do not visit the list of Farmers' Mar-kets advertising free-range meat she printed out.

Then there is the new way she thinks of her body, as a ma-chine with dietary requirements; the new way she thinks of food, as molecules of sustenance with this or that protein, this or that amount of iron. She learns the word haemoglobin in a new way, *haem and non-haem sources of iron*. She learns that green leafy vegetables should be ingested along with something containing Vitamin C: toma-toes or orange juice. She buys nuts and dried fruit. She sees her doctor and has a blood test. She goes on an iron supplement. All the while Elizabeth monitors her energy levels: today vitality! tomorrow weari-ness. Today weight loss! tomorrow regained. She spends time perus-ing the health food section at the supermarket, *organic* and *soy-based*, exciting new words finding their way into her trolley. Soy sausages, soy-based vegie-mince, soy-based vegetarian sausage-roll mixture, just add water! Sanitarium brand, with its wholesome green packag-ing, provides her with interesting new meal ideas. She buys polenta, wholemeal spaghetti, brown organic rice, muesli, natural yoghurt, lentils, beans, bushels of spinach, bok choy, cabbage and broccoli. Then she eats, stuffs her face, cooks and eats and then cooks more.

Elizabeth's cat was a Christmas present from her parents. They knew it would be a Big Change, she and her partner, when they went to the Lost Dogs and Cats Home to pick her out. If they wanted to go away, could they find someone to feed the cat? Would the cat take to its kitty litter? Would the landlord let them have a cat and under what conditions? Would they have enough money for food, vet check-ups, worming tablets, flea treatments, let alone a bed, a food dish, a litter tray, a scratching-post, a pet-carrier and toys? Yes, yes, yes, yes, they said. When Elizabeth saw her (they didn't know yet that her name would be Hazelnut) she knew immediately that this kitten was to be their kitten. She was the first in a row of cages. She put up her little paws and scratched them through the bars, drawing first blood.

The kitten slid on the tile floors, a tiny creature in a vast place. Elizabeth followed her around, fascinated. Later, when Elizabeth stopped eating meat, and Hazelnut became the only meat-eater in the household, she knew it had not happened, not really, because of Peter Singer or her wish to be good. She stopped eating meat because of cats.

There have always been cats. Growing up in Adelaide there was Sophie, a thin tabby who fell pregnant and gave birth in Elizabeth's baby brother's cot. Elizabeth's parents woke them in the middle of the night and they gathered, sleepily, around the cot where three blind kittens were sighing and fumbling for their mother's teat. There was a black one, a male, and two female tabbies, so each child had a corresponding cat. The black one was Joe's, her baby brother's and it was named Edward; her sister had Cuddlepie, named after May Gibbs's gumnut, and Elizabeth had Sunshine, a fluffy little tabby who ran about madly and didn't come inside at night. Edward and his mother died soon after one another, she of age, he hit by a car. Elizabeth wasn't too upset by the deaths, heaven being a word spoken daily in the household, not only on special occasions.

And she had Sunshine, with whom she could talk.

She had realised the phenomenon one morning when she and Sunshine were playing in the backyard where some white plants were growing. Elizabeth and her sister dared each other to eat the plants.

They ate all kinds of things based on these challenges: snails, passion-fruit skins, grass, pebbles, and these weeds were no different; in any case they dripped an appetising white fluid onto their hands. Just before Elizabeth ate the plant, she looked at Sunshine and knew quite clearly that her cat didn't want her to eat it. Later when she and her sister turned rashy-red and spasmodically vomited the milkweed into two bowls, Elizabeth remembered Sunshine's warning and vowed to listen to her cat-instinct more often. After that, Elizabeth spoke to her cat regularly, just as she spoke with people, but without opening her mouth. Sunshine told her if she wanted anything, and Elizabeth told Sunshine what she could do about it. Sunshine advised her on matters of safety in the yard, Elizabeth warned Sunshine from the road, where her little brother had been killed as a kitten. Nothing separated them; they looked at the other's quiet face, and knew, knew *exactly*, what to do.

She still remembers the time when she realised she could no longer understand Sunshine. It was during the weeks leading up to the family's move interstate. Many things were crowding Elizabeth's mind, and her cat no longer found a space in her senses. Later, a psychology-student friend would explain the thing as a loss of certainty due to the adult awakening in the child; a realisation that what once seemed an indisputable reality was now as rocky, as unstable an event as the idea of 'home', the idea of 'family.' When the day came for them to move, Sunshine couldn't be found. They called for her, but had to leave, in the end, to drive the nine hours by nightfall. Elizabeth never saw her cat again, but held her there in Adelaide, as a picture of the surety of miracles she could once claim.

Recently, Elizabeth has been quietly outraged by a series of commercials on TV and in newspapers funded by the Red Meat Council of Australia. In them it is jocularly asserted by a respected Australian actor, that eating red meat is not only essential for one's health and vitality, but unarguably natural, the outcome of a series of evolutionary betterments of the human race. If one doesn't eat it "three to four times a week," the implication is that one is unnatural, backward, lacklustre, probably ill, more than likely stupid, with a small undeveloped brain. She does not begrudge people their meat, does not issue disgust or judgement upon meateaters whom she loves, not even her brother-in-law, part of whose farm is devoted to the raising of beef-cattle. But to justify it with these false threads of logic, aggressively claiming a sort of muscly superiority over the animal kingdom… it turns her stomach. But she tries to hide it, outrage not being in her character.

She watches her cat Hazelnut crunching through a bowl of dried pellets, made undoubtedly from the stuff leftover from the slaughterhouse floor, dried, compressed, coloured and jammed with vitamins.

'Did you know Peter Singer feeds his cat tofu?' she asks her partner as they watch Hazelnut, like parents watching the strange habits of a new child.

He laughs, 'Really? That's going a bit far, isn't it?'

She nods, 'I mean it's natural for a cat – she has hunting claws and teeth – to be carnivorous. Weren't they always that way?'

But Sam Neill, on the television, also talks about teeth, molars for tearing flesh from bone. What is this *natural* she speaks of?

How, then, does she live with this contradiction? She does not eat meat because it would be like, *just like*, eating the flesh of her cat, a creature she loves, whose pain or death would be something of unconscionable sadness, whose *being* seems to have, although it does not sound reasonable, as much importance as her own. And yet her cat has no qualms at all about catching a mouse or a butterfly, and not just killing it, nor eating it, but *torturing* it: catching it, clawing at it, letting it go, then chasing and catching it again, until the thing dies of fear and exhaustion. Should she teach her cat morals? Should she feed it tofu, or lentil burgers, tell it *no!* when it catches a mouse? And if she doesn't, isn't that an admission that she, Elizabeth, is the superior being, able to overcome her evolution-made instincts for something more cerebral, an idea that eating meat is unnecessary? Gently, Elizabeth picks up the bird Hazelnut offers, caught dexterously despite the warning bell around her neck. The bird's heart is quivering; it has lost feathers and is bleeding a little. In the firm pocket Elizabeth has made of her hands, the bird is still and quiet, and does fly away after a few reeling steps through the grass. 'It will be alright,' Elizabeth tells herself, and looks at her cat, who is mourning the inexplicable loss of her prize by racing about and sniffing at the fallen down which litters the floor.

Short Fiction

The Nature of It

> *'No one else could ever be admitted here, since this gate was made*
> *only for you. I am now going to shut it.'*
> – Kafka, 'Before the Law'

The boy's head hits the road while his foot is still caught in the sliding tram door. The ticket inspectors, a group of three, had cornered him there, but now bark out at the driver, *Stop the tram. Open the door. He's stuck.* Their voices already betraying that animal: self-preservation. The boy's foot is tugged free and he yelps weakly before sinking into unconsciousness, blood slowly gliding from his head down Lonsdale Street. The tram remains stationary, all its doors agape, its lights blinking in astonishment.

For a minute Garrett can hardly move. He's looked too late and missed, except from the corner of his eye, the accident. The incident with the inspectors was a common enough scene – the three of them signalling each other and gathering around a fare-evader who stuttered an excuse about not having the change. Garrett hadn't bothered to observe. But this, the voices gave it away – that creature *instinct* breaking through – was something out of the ordinary. The female onlookers, *Oh my GOD!* already touching the safety of their wedding rings or phones. The men gruffly moving towards the action, giving orders. The tram inspectors themselves, turning white, banding shoulder to shoulder, their backs to the crowd. It's something he already knows he'll read versions of in the newspaper. The excuses will be parleyed back and forth. The boy: I tried to explain that the money must have fallen out of this hole in my pocket; (photo with caption:

He needed this like a hole in the…). The ticket inspectors: We did our job to the letter of our training. At not one moment were we in physical contact with the kid. Garrett hears them both and doesn't try to take sides. He fully understands the situation of each party.

And, for the moment, here is something that would make a perfect excuse for why he is late for work. He could rush into the office, turn the radio on where the accident is just beginning to be reported. I was on that tram, he could say a little breathlessly to the stern face of the Boss. I had to walk. 'Where's your bloody car,' the Boss might ask, reasonably. 'I don't drive,' he would reply, and explain: 'environment'. We are all the same, Garrett thinks heavily as he rises from his seat to leave the evacuated tram. Excuse-makers, blame-pointers. The ambulance and the boy's mother will be arriving soon. A gash in the head looks worse than it is. The lives of these people – these people he can understand so well, so easily – will continue after some kind of recompense. It is a story he knows very well, he hears it every day in the courtroom. He tells it every night again at his desk with this new hobby of his – crime writing. Imagining the lives of others is now his business, just like imagining he has a Boss to report to, when really there is no Boss but himself. He reports to himself – there was an accident, I had to walk – and lets himself off gently.

In the anteroom of the chambers Garrett arranges his wig and robes. In the mirror his face is like something out of historical portraiture: the weary judge. Not worn down, as it would be poignantly implied in the oil-colour, by the weight of the world's ills, the weight of his profession. He's actually exhausted because of something much more frivolous – a late night spent making up a grisly story for readers of paperback fiction. His first novel had been a mild success; he'd published it pseudonymously, despite the beseeching of his agent who knew Garrett's identity as a Melbourne Supreme Court judge would earn him the edge of credibility that would make the novel, _____, stand out. The agent had also advised him to create an idiosyncratic detective character who could star in a series of novels, but this advice too Garrett chose to disregard. The second novel began from scratch with a new scenario and a new cast of the same old characters: criminal, detective, lawyer. The crimes, of course, were heinous and diverse, the criminal a clever unloved maniac. Inevitably, small elements of cases he'd prosecuted and judged over the years had found their way into his writing, but dolled up and dramatised, cleaned, placed carefully amongst a nest of clues. This was to be expected, said his agent, after all our experiences are all we have to work with. And our imagination, Garrett had corrected him, our experiences and our imagination.

He glances again over the brief for today's case and then enters the familiar trappings of the courtroom. The announcement of his entry rings out and everyone shuffles to rise and then sit. To his left the jury and in front, the defence, the prosecution.

The young man on trial, a Mr Langland, looks vaguely familiar. He is looking hard at Garrett, as though he too recognises something, but then as the charges are read out, his eyes dip to the table in front of him. Breaking and entering, assault, murder in the first degree. The round of statements, witnesses and cross-questioning begins and to Garrett's eyes the case seems fairly open and shut. The man will get thirty years at least. For a moment Garrett, and he considers this permissible in a situation where he plays, practically, a passive role, is distracted from the details. He sees the boy from the tram this morning and the group that framed him. The tram driver, whose foot had been on the pedal that closed the door that etc. The inspectors whose intimidating attentions had made the boy nervous which caused him to lose balance which then led to etc. The house that Jack built ended in a tangle of lines of causality. Garrett prided himself on tracing them all. He had done it as a young lawyer and he did it now in his books. A story is never straight, he thinks, there are always loops and sideways turns, like that old string-trick the fishnet. But at that moment, cutting through his musings, someone to his left says, *I had no choice. We live in a country and under a law that offers choice as a democratic right. But is there room in the law for a man with no choices left?* It is Langland in the witness box, looking straight at Garrett, uttering the words Garrett had written only hours earlier in his study in his house in his quiet dark street.

Langland turns and continues. His lawyer prompts him with congenial questions. But for Garrett the world discontinues. I had a late night, he thinks, and I'm old, very old, and getting older. His age, for once, soothes him; the weight of those years bearing down on his head like a poultice. My God I must stay alert, he thinks, the doddery old fool is knocking at my door, coming to replace me! He almost chuckles at himself.

For the rest of the day, everything is as usual. Over dinner, Garrett tells his literary agent of the strange incident. The agent relates the story of a famous author he once handled who became so immersed in a novel he was writing that he lived for a week under the illusion that he *was* the main character. 'Who happened to be a nineteenth-century hangman,' giggles the agent. 'Now *that* was a week difficult to explain.' Garrett goes home to his desk and erases the line about choices which he thought was a little grandiose anyway. Once again, he continues writing into the small hours. If he stops he knows he will wonder what else there is to do.

Prosecution is on the telephone early the next morning to let him know that new evidence has come to light in the Langland case, asking whether this new information can be brought into the courtroom. He tells prosecution to meet him at the office in an hour. 'Tell defence to come,' he says, his eyes still creaky with sleep.

In his office, prosecution is animated, on her feet and pacing. 'We've just realised,' she says, 'that Langland's murder has a strong connection with two other unsolved murders in different states.' What is that strong connection, Garrett asks. 'The murder victims are all elderly women, widows, and well off. On its own this is not so unusual, but there is something else.' I see, says Garrett, his throat clenching. Go on. 'The victims were all killed in the same way. They were seated and bound and then strangled from behind with something quite soft, judging from the minimal grazing and bruising.' Garrett's head is reeling, his hands tremble as he casts about for water to unfasten his claggy throat. Does the method have a particular significance to the offender's profile? he chokes. 'Our criminal psychologist says the deliberation with which the victim was prepared suggests a cold-blooded crime, but the relatively gentle binding and 'soft' strangulation suggests an element of compassion.' Garrett's head is in his hands. Yes, yes, that seems quite feasible, he says quietly. For today, I will allow the case to be postponed while you gather more information about the... And question the... Langland. Pose him further questions. Thank you, you can go.

Prosecution and defence leave and Garrett crumples in his chair. But I made that up! he thinks, in despair. The old lonely women, the binding, the crime of pity. The implication of a collusion between killer and killed. Not just a crime book, but a psychological drama, that's how it was to be pitched. I must have heard of those other two murders, he thinks. Even sealed cases leak to judges. It must have reached my ears and I used it, thinking it original. I am memory-logged after all, he thinks. Perhaps my imagination has been appropriated by memory. Perhaps it's squashed in a corner. He sighs and realises a whole chunk of his book will have to be revised. He also realises his day is free, yawns in front of him.

He calls his agent and they meet for breakfast. Garrett explains the new circumstances. 'What an annoying twist of fate,' his agent sighs. 'It'll be all over the papers soon enough, you'll have to deviate from the original plan.' Yes I know, says Garrett. I feel like my ideas are drying up. It's like they're already old when I write them down. 'It's the nature of it,' says his agent. Garrett doesn't know whether he means the nature of the genre or the plain nature of life itself. On his way home, he decides he must push on straight away – get over this new hurdle before it begins to fester in his mind. Something catches his eye from a café by the roadside and he swivels abruptly, knocking a man back with his elbow. It is Langland, he is sure of it, sitting with a mug of coffee in his hand, staring right at him. Sorry, Garrett mutters, and the man he knocked raises his eyebrows. He glances back at the café and somehow already knows that this time Langland won't be there.

Am I so lonely, Garrett thinks when he arrives home, that madness must descend so quickly? His wife's death, over two years ago now, had caused a flurry, the ripples of which were only now beginning to disappear from view. His two children had arrived from afar to attend to matters, and to him. Seeing him back in the judge's seat and with a new 'pastime' as they called it, they had left, with brisk promises to return by Christmas. It was at their insistence that he'd stayed in the big quiet house. And only now its silence has become a thing to be avoided, Garrett realises, at all costs. I begin at the end of the story – when the maniac divulges the revelation sweet-talked out of him by the detective. Then I retrace my steps to the beginning, around all the loops, contorting myself through the twists, to arrive at a hazy morning, blank like this one. That's when the keys fall quiet, the sentences stop scrolling up the page, and I turn the machine off, flinching at the echo of each slippered footstep on the way to bed. Three hours of exhausted sleep later and I've accounted for all the barbed and poisoned minutes this house can pitch.

And now this. This Langland, who reminds him of someone he can only have met in the dead of night, on the scrolling page.

Unless there is some other explanation, Garrett thinks, his lawyer's mind awakening as the sun heads towards its zenith. *If I am indeed still sane, then Langland and I have a connection, something that has stayed coiled in my memory for a long time. The widows, and that troubled stare, where did I see them? Was it in a dream? One of those dyed dreams that leaves a permanent tint on the sand of memory? Or was it something simpler, a film?* Hitchcock's *Shadow of a Doubt*, and *Rope* too, *is that where Langland comes from? The clever killer, the killer with a paradigm, like Raskolnikov in the St Petersburg thriller,* Crime and Punishment. *The criminal with a reasonable argument, a Jean Valjean, a Robin Hood. Are these Langland's models?* Garrett halts himself. *My models too,* he thinks, *Langland's and mine both.* Garrett fumbles for his desk chair and sits in front of the screen. The ending of the book is yet to flash across his mind as it usually does, like a flightpath made bright by thunderstrike. He thinks of the tram yesterday morning, and the people whose thoughts he felt he could read. *We are all the same,* he remembers thinking, and now revises, *I make everyone the same, they are all me,* before switching off the blank screen and leaving the house.

*

Langland's hands seek out each other as he sits and waits in the cell.

Finally it is happening, he thinks. *Finally the word will ring out,* guilty, *and I will know. I will know for sure. Even though it feels like a request and then a response, between glances, among eyes... I will know there was no request, there was only me, there was only action: response.*

He stands and shakes his body, his hands gripping his wrists where the cuffs had been. *All I know is being necessary,* he thinks. *This thing I can do when no-one can. This* thing, *I should call a crime now. Now that I know.*

He revisits, as he often does, the memories of Angela, Joyce and Carlotta, whose silent pleas he had recognised. Who had found in him the reply they pined for. Who had sought him, defined him. Who had asked the question only he could answer, *Yes*. And again he thanks them with blessings, *without you I would be nothing*.

And once again he is nothing.

Langland looks upon himself as if from a great distance. He is simply the criminal, having nothing but the crime to describe him. It is rare, he thinks, for the criminal to reappear after he has been caught once, and confessed. That is the end of him. Criminals have only one story: once it is told, they disappear. While the hero may return, may reroute his white horse and ride through the town again.

Langland thinks of the judge, in whom he had recognised the same request as the women. He remembers the moment: their eyes meet and together they see the depth of their terrible need.

*

At the tram stop Garrett leaves a message on his agent's phone: I'm scrapping the book; it isn't going anywhere. He boards the tram and sits opposite two young backpackers who are holding their tram tickets between two fingers, examining them. A woman gets on and talks loudly to the tram-driver before heading up the aisle, asking people for change. Garrett gives her a two-dollar coin which she drops into a dirty glove, barely looking at him. An elderly couple speak to each other in Dutch and clutch their bags when the glove woman walks by. '*Nay*,' they say, and shake their heads. These people, thinks Garrett, I could gather them up like chicks they are so familiar.

Langland, too, is familiar. Garrett tests his imagination: Langland in a cell, reflecting. Is this also something I have seen before? he wonders, and tests it again: Langland reflecting on his crimes. Garrett sees it clearly and quietly celebrates. He tests it further: myself arriving at Langland's cell.

He arrives at the remand centre near the courts, a temporary jail for those on trial. 'Another visitor!' yells the officer to Langland as Garrett enters. 'God!' Langland calls from within. 'He's had people in all morning,' says the officer. 'It's a new case now, seems like.' Garrett murmurs a noise and signs his name before being led into the cell block. Handcuffed, Langland walks in front of him to the meeting room where a guard stands by the door for their interview.

Langland looks at Garrett across the table with the same familiar stare as at their first meeting. Why do you look at me in that way? asks Garrett. Langland says nothing for a while, then, 'I recog-nise you.' Yes, says Garrett, me too. They are quiet. The old women you killed, Garrett begins, and Langland stiffens. Did they say any-thing to you when you broke into their houses? The guard releases his hands from behind his back and lets them hang by his sides, fingers ready to grip and charge. Langland looks away. 'No,' he says. 'They were mostly quiet. Sometimes they offered me money or jewellery.' Were they afraid? asks Garrett. 'Yes, but everyone is afraid before they die.' Langland looks at Garrett again. 'What else do you want to know?' he asks. I want to know… Garrett stops and falls silent. Did they understand? he tries again. Those women, did they understand? It is the wrong question, but he asks it, procrastinating, like the inspec-tors from yesterday, as they huddled in a grim circle. 'Oh yes, they understood,' says Langland, as Garrett knew he would. 'They under-stood me more than I understand myself.' Yes, says Garrett.

He rises to leave and looks once more at Langland, pleading with him silently. With a nod, Langland indicates that he compre-hends, then bows his head, heavily as though weighted with rocks. Garrett leaves him sitting there at the table, and goes home to wait.

Museum

You have to enter a dark place to come in here.

If you are in a room full of light (the wood is pine, the cushions are plump and blue) then wait until night-time when there is lamplight leaning over your shoulder and shadows on the wall. It's not to set the mood; it's just if you wake up from a nightmare in the daytime, you feel somehow betrayed by light.

I went back to the Adelaide Museum. It was the fifth step on my 'Road to Recovery'. Everything was the same – the massive model of the blue whale hanging from cords in the front window; the ill-lit corridor of stuffed animals behind glass and ropes: bears, kangaroos, bats, panthers. The blue room of fish with the model sting-ray in the back corner. Its false eyes. And the insect room.

My father, one day, refused to come in with us. Except he didn't *refuse* since there were no questions or pleading, he just sat outside and said, 'I'll wait for you,' and Mum said, 'He doesn't like to see the dead animals.' We stepped in that day feeling guilty, but wanting so much to wander and look and be frightened and safe at the same time. Feeling guilty, as though we had shot all the animals and shoved our hands filled with chemicals and stuffing down their throats to fill out their dead paws and ears.

There were a lot of people there that day, parents who had read the 'Ten free things to do with your kids during the holidays' article in the paper and had come for the 2pm cardboard mask-making session, like us. I made a lion face with the same colour scheme I used for my pictures of the sun: red tapering inwards from orange to yellow blended with my fingers dipped in coloured shavings. I cut the edges of my paper plate into spiky triangles and drew a cat's mouth and whiskers. Mum jabbed the scissors through the lion's eyes and I stuck an icy-pole stick on the back to hold it up to my face. I looked out through the ragged holes at the other masks.

A lion, I looked around the room and saw the man then for the first time. He was in blue overalls on a ladder with his back to the long table. He was replacing a light. He had taken a section of the ceiling out and was pulling different coloured wires together into a bunch. He looked like my Dad because he had a beard and a slim strength. So when he looked over at me and waved, I waved back and took the lion's mask off. He made a gesture like he was roaring and clawing at something, then he laughed and went back to the broken light.

We talked with the other children, my sister won a prize for her gorilla mask, and then Mum said, 'Let's go see the rest and then go back to Dad.' I looked for the man in overalls before we left the room, but only his ladder was there.

The insect room was my favourite. There were desks lining the walls with little black boxes for small people to stand on so they could see. The desks were covered in glass beneath which were rows of butter-flies, moths, beetles and spiders each with a pin through the abdomen, their wings and legs spread wide. Beneath every one was a tiny label with the Latin and common names. I loved to pronounce the Latin words in their stylish italic: *Parnassius phoebus, Morpho granadensis*. On one wall was an exhibit on lepidopterists – old photos of men in veiled hats, their pants tucked into socks, running through fields with bloated nets billowing behind them. There was a butterfly net on dis-play which I always imagined was exactly like the one Roald Dahl's BFG used to catch dreams from sleeping children's breath.

Mum and my sister didn't like the insect room. It made me proud to linger bravely over the wolf spiders and elephant beetles, while they looked cursorily at the pretty butterflies and caterpillars. They wan-dered into the plants and trees room which adjoined the insect room and which was the last room before the exit. I stayed gazing into the live ant farm. I watched the little insects scurry around their maze as though they were two feet under normal tree-fed earth instead of four feet above-ground in carefully chemically enhanced soil with conven-iently placed food scraps.

The man caught me by surprise when he grabbed me from behind with a hand over my mouth and the other arm under my legs, picking me up off the floor before I could gasp.

And of course I know now that this was the first violence done to me: taking away my body's and my mind's ability to comprehend. It wasn't that I couldn't scream, it was more that I couldn't remember how.

He took me to a dark place.

Somehow he got inside the museum walls where we climbed a ladder up into an attic area which was mostly rafters. Some parts, though, had sturdy boards running the length. He put me down here and stopped for a while, listening and breathing. I realised this was where the man had been fixing the light before, above the mask-making room. There were electrical cables running along boards up into the roof.

He turned to look at me from where he was crouching and smiled. He waved and growled at me.

'You remember me?'

I had heard about Strangers in social ed. class at school. *If someone talks to you in a way that makes you uncomfortable just say 'No!' and run away. If a man says 'Get in the car' just shout 'No!' and run away. If someone hugs you or kisses you in a way that you don't like just shout 'NO!' Run away.*

I did not shout No! I was trembling from head to toe, crouching on the boards, looking past the man at the ladder.

'You're the lion.'

The man didn't look like my Dad this close. His beard was shorter and rounder, my Dad's was long and pointy like a wizard's. The man was shorter too and his skin was very white.

'The police won't find us here. Your Mum and Dad won't find us here. It's such a secret place no-one will ever find us.'

I was crying quietly and thought I would start screaming. I opened my mouth, but the man crept quickly over to me with something in his hand. He pressed it against my knee and I felt a jolt through my body that landed in my teeth.

'You see this? It's an electric current. If you scream I'll buzz you with it, I'll sting you with it like a bee, okay? So you have to be quiet, because it hurts.'

I was a protected child compared with my schoolmates who used words I had never heard and were told off for them. I watched half an hour of TV a day and read Roald Dahl and C.S. Lewis books at night. The shock of the electric jolt came as less of a surprise to me as the fact that he had arranged such a simple set of conditions for my capture. I had never seen on TV or on a movie the playing out of a 'hostage situation' or a kidnapping for ransom situation. I had no idea of their workings. I had never heard of silence being exchanged for a lack of pain. Such a quick and brutal punishment for such an unfair reason. I was petrified by this man and his buzzing logic.

The man sat behind me and pulled me up onto his lap. He was still very quiet and tense, listening for sounds of disturbance. He absently bobbed me up and down on his legs, which made me think later that he probably did this with children of his own. I thought of the word *dandled* which I had read recently and had asked Mum what it meant. To me it was, and is now doubly so, a sinister word, a mixture of *dandy* and *handled*, a toying and petting.

'In the jungle, the quiet jungle, the lion sleeps tonight.'

The man stopped singing and listened again. We could hear voices from below.

'Katie? Katie, sweetie, where are you?'

Mum had a hard edge at the back of her voice and I knew that she thought I'd just wandered off, but that she was also beginning to run through the other possibilities in her mind. I feel sick now when I think about what my parents went through at this time. It seems to me there are few things worse than not knowing where a loved one is. It is a certain kind of helpless panic which will die down in stages into a weary frozenness, but will then flare up again in countless images, all violent, terrifying and black.

'Katie? Is that your name? Katie-girl? Katie-lion?'

'Mum-mum-mum,' I whispered, my skin still humming from the electricity. 'I want my Mum.'

'Listen to me, Katie-lion. Sometimes you gotta love other people too. Your Mum is going to be ok, and you're going to forget about her for a bit. Just think about being up here with me. You can go back to your Mum after that.'

I ran my phone number and address over in my head. *337 4621, 7 Karyn Avenue Campbelltown, oh-positive blood, Mum and Dad are Jackie and Wes.*

The voices went away and the man relaxed. He began to rub the material of my skirt and T-shirt between his finger and thumb. Then he put his hands under my T-shirt and against the skin of my belly.

'No!' I said as loudly as I dared, my heart pounding blood through my ears. 'I don't like that.'

The man took his hands away and picked up the broken electric cable. He gripped my hand and slowly brought the fizzing cable down on my palm. He held it there for five, ten seconds.

'Stop telling me what to do,' said the man after he had taken the cord away and I had finished crying. The hairs on my arms and legs were standing straight up, I could see lights behind my eyeballs. I concentrated on keeping entirely still.

We sat in silence for a while, listening as a growing number of footsteps began pattering along the floorboards beneath us. 'Kate!' I heard my father say. I had a ridiculous mental image of him searching for me while shielding his eyes with one hand, trying not to look at the stuffed animals.

'Kate! Katie!' These were unfamiliar voices now, probably museum staff or visitors. I heard my name called again and again over the loudspeaker system. I heard my sister start to cry and missed her terribly.

'It's too noisy here,' the man said, but he didn't move.

*

I have heard and read that psychopaths, that word casually bandied about in action flicks and ghost stories, are characterised primarily by a diminished sense of social responsibility and an inability to establish deep human relationships. Symptoms or signs of psychopathic behaviour often emerge early in a child's life, with stealing, truanting and causing harm to animals. Usually an individual can be linked to some kind of trauma experienced during childhood which then develops into a cycle of hostility and rejection as he no longer expects acceptance or fulfilment from social interaction. The psychopath can also be recognised on a physical level by a brain abnormality. I read all this much later, not in the obsessive way some 'victims' do when they try to understand exactly what was happening to them in their tormentor's mind; not even in the way some parents do when they discover their child to have a disease and want to be able to discuss its possibilities intelligently with a doctor. I read it because the language soothed me.

The sentences were encyclopaedic: succinct and well-rounded, full of other words you could look up in the same encyclopaedia, until you fully understood them. The books gave me examples of situations which might generate psychopathic behaviour and I imagined John Harrison, my captor, to have experienced every one of them. I imagined him wetting the bed and waking drenched and stinking in the night, only to rouse his angry drunk father. I imagined him at school, not being able to concentrate because he had been awake all night from being beaten by his father, or trying to protect his mother from being killed. I imagined his teachers and schoolmates, derisive, losing patience with his slowness. I imagined him then becoming hostile towards any kind of interaction. The first impression he now gives to new students or teachers is one of deliberate antagonism and aggression, even though this behaviour has been built up over years. I imagine his father's brain to have a slight abnormality due to *his* own disturbed and abusive childhood and for this abnormality to have been passed on and exacerbated through mistreatment. I imagine John Harrison's brain – lopsided and slightly blackened with some essential part missing.

I imagine him tearing the wings from flies and the legs from grasshoppers, throwing rocks at cats and not feeding his dog. I imagine him hitting people younger and weaker than himself. He leaves school early, becomes involved with other boys like him, starts stealing cars and robbing Seven Elevens. He can't find a job. He becomes a loner, believes himself to be worthless and believes the rest of the world to be hateful. He starts drinking and taking drugs. His involvements with women are violent, short and loveless. One girl gets pregnant and he gives her money now and then when she hassles him about their five-year-old son. He is assigned a work-for-the-dole project at the local museum and occasionally turns up. I was John Harrison's first serious offence.

Imagining John Harrison's life in this way soothes me. It makes the electric jolt of my hours with him explainable, cushioned by their inevitability. People don't understand when I say this to them; they say, 'You can be angry. There is nothing you have to forgive.' They say, 'He took something away from you. Now justice will take something away from him. Then you can move on.' They all use this term 'moving on' as though I am on a train or walking along a footpath and I have stopped because there is something terrible in my way. This dreadful slow process they all speak of, a matter of lifting one's foot and stepping over the mess, or finding a way around it, and then taking a step along the path you were on before. And then walking, chugging along, until the terrible thing is so far away it is out of sight.

But really, it is as though I have picked the terrible thing up in my arms and veered off on a different track and I'm riding with it by my side.

*

The Scar

He wakes up tracing a scar above his eyebrow with a finger. He touches it like it's a track, back and forth along its length. Still half-dreaming his finger is a vehicle, and the scar its journey.

In the mirror, the scar doesn't go away. It rises unmistakeably from the flesh, gleams silver in the light. The scar extends diagonally from his eyebrow, giving him a shrewd look; quizzical is the word. But mockingly so.

From his office he calls his doctor friend.

'How quickly can a scar form from a cut?' he asks.

He learns that after the initial laceration it depends on a few things. Exposure to the air, bacteria, sunlight. The cut needs to go through stages of scabbing. The cells need to regenerate. White scar tissue will form on a deep cut, so the process will usually take at least a week.

His friend pauses. She is the kind of person who likes to finish things with a review. 'Once the scar tissue has formed, it is as though that part of your skin is dead. There is no more shedding of cells, no regeneration. The scar is a permanent seal.'

He hangs up, runs a hand through his hair, turns back to the computer.

At his mother's for dinner, he checks himself again in the bathroom. Even when he relaxes all his facial muscles, it still looks as though he is asking a question. His brother and sister are also there, with their partners and children. After he kisses his sister, she holds his elbows to look at his face. He looks back. 'What?' she snaps eventually.

The kids pile onto his legs and demand he pull coins from their ears. The others regroup in the kitchen. He's The Single Uncle at family gatherings, and takes the role genially. The children don't look at him strangely, but as they always do: greedily, their mouths gaping into smiles.

His mother always makes roast lamb for them, the potatoes seasoned with rosemary. She makes little plates with oven-bake potato gems for the children, with greens on the side. For the youngest child, she cuts beans into bite-sizes. 'I can do that, Mum,' says his brother, from his chair. She doesn't reply, and they continue eating.

'Remember when you got your scar, Michael?'

He starts. Potato falls from his fork to the floor.

His mother is kneeling beside the children's table, while they squeal at her, refusing to eat.

'I remember,' says Linny. 'It was that night when–'

'Brodie put that down right now!' His brother Andrew is already on his feet, tossing his napkin down, smacking the toy from his son's hand. Linny goes back to eating. Michael and his mother gaze down as Andrew reprimands Brodie, until the boy's face flattens and trembles into angry fear. Michael catches his nephew's eye, tries to wink secretly, but Brodie is facing his plate, and stabbing potato gems with a fork.

His mother must brace herself against the table to stand slowly, and holds it to catch her breath before she takes her seat beside Linny. The children eat quietly, and the adults sip their wine.

'Mum, you and I were in the sewing room, trying to make that goddamned seaweed costume, remember?' Linny says.

'Lin. Just,' Andrew indicates the children, 'watch the mouth.'

Linny pauses, her fork halfway to her mouth.

'It was an underwater theme school concert,' says his mother. 'Your class sang 'Yellow Submarine,' didn't they?'

'Mhmm,' Linny nods with her mouth full. 'Four of the boys got to be the Beatles. The rest of us were just octopuses and seaweed. And we were making that da-, the costume, out of old stockings stuffed with newspaper!' Linny holds her face in her hands, heaving with laughter.

'It was all we had!'

'All the other kids came with these elaborate things with crepe paper and cellophane,' Linny shrieks. 'And here I am in a garbage-sack with socks poking out of my sides!' She chokes with laughter, and his mother smiles. Michael puts his hand to his eyebrow, and chuckles, observing.

'Then we heard this yell from the–'

'For God's sake, son!'

Brodie has spilled his water all over the children's table, onto his plate of food and down the front of his pants. He pushes his chair back and stares at the drip. The other children are giggling, and picking up their plates.

Michael's mother gets paper towels and cloths, kneels on the floor to wipe it. Andrew grabs his son by the arm and hauls him to the lounge. Everyone gets up to try and help. Dishes clatter, the children start running around. Michael cleans Brodie's plate and fixes him more food. Then retreats to the bathroom.

In the mirror the scar is like a shaft of light, glimmering against the metal. It cuts through the top of his eyebrow, making him look disjointed, half-finished. When he touches it, the feeling is only half-there, originating in his finger, then dying upon the scar's white seal. Like that old joke about the patient who feels pains wherever she touches, and is diagnosed with a broken finger.

Brodie is back in his chair, sullenly staring ahead, not touching his plate. Andrew eats in wrenching motions, gathering a forkful of bits and pieces, smoothing the sides with his knife, before plunging it towards his mouth.

Linny and his mother are discussing a movie they saw. Michael sips his wine, makes faces at the children. Everything is hushed; the quiet tinker of cutlery against crockery, the murmur of voices, the children's faces smeared, their movements awkward.

'Me and Michael were in the loungeroom playing Body Boggle,' says Andrew, his voice suddenly an authority in the room.

'Oh I remember that game, like Twister but with the alphabet,' says Linny, looking again at Michael, her gaze lingering above his eye.

'Yeah. With only two people you were supposed to only spell out the short words, but we always tried to do the long ones. The ones you're meant to have five people for.'

Michael looks at his brother, and can remember the new plastic smell of the Boggle mat, and the feel of it under his sweaty palm, creased plastic sliding across the carpet.

'I don't remember the word we were spelling that day, do you, Mike? But it was one of the really long ones, like… trigonometry or something.'

Andrew has the room now, even the children are looking at him, his son listening to the strange lilt in his father's voice.

'We didn't just use our hands and feet, we used our heads too, to get more letters, sometimes even our fingers.'

The feeling of the games returns to Michael, the sweat and the tension, the wait while his older brother chose a word, then the sick feeling in his stomach when the four syllables were pronounced. He always knew what Andrew would say next: 'You can use your freaky bones, Mikey.' And would sneer.

Michael had been born with hips-joints that bent backwards, and had spent most of his toddler years in a brace, he'd seen the photos. As a result his hips were still slightly double-jointed – he could even do the horizontal splits if he wanted – but to hold them backward like this became unbearably painful, his torso thrust outwards, his spine curving unnaturally.

But this was the challenge the boys set for themselves. Five-person words with only two people and their wayward limbs.

'So we started to make the word. It always took a few tries before we figured out the best way to do it. We'd disregard the order of the letters and just group them according to where they were placed on the mat.'

Michael remembers this too, and knew it was cheating the rules of the game, which he had read meticulously. But Andrew was adept in the ways of cutting time, and managing space. It was the kind of skill with economy that led him into the world of business technology, managing computer space to achieve the greatest output. Even then, he did it deftly, with a kind of grace, scanning the Boggle mat of letters, grouping the squares into manageable blocks.

Michael's mother gets up to clear the dishes, and the brothers vaguely protest. It is as though she does not hear them, and continues gathering forks, and knives, glasses and dirty plates. She orders them by the sink, fills it with water, begins scrubbing quickly, like a bird, her back bent. She turns to face them, suds dripping from the cloth to the floor. 'Linny and I, we were in the other room.'

There is a silence, Michael and Andrew keep their eyes on the table, Linny is picking up crumbs with her finger. 'Yeah we were in the sewing room,' she says eventually. Michael's mother turns back to the sink, her arms in motion like machines.

'We heard this thud and a crash, and then Michael screaming. Mum you had pins in your mouth, remember, and afterwards we realised one had cut the inside of your cheek.'

'I didn't feel it,' says his mother, her back to them.

The children come in with a DVD they want to watch, and Michael sets it up for them. They gather on the couch like one being, their arms and legs entwine loosely, their eyes glaze, their mouths limp ovals as they gaze at the screen.

There is a silence when Michael returns to the kitchen. Andrew goes to the fridge for beer. Linny looks up and smiles.

'What do you remember, Mike?' she asks. 'Do you remember the fall, or the ambulance ride or anything?'

They all turn to look at him. 'No,' he says, 'nothing like that.' He sits.

'Well you had concussion,' says Linny quietly, still looking steadily at him.

'To be honest, I don't remember anything.'

Andrew turns his beer bottle around and around on the table.

'It's never come back to you?' he asks. 'In flashbacks, nothing?'

Michael looks at them all. 'Nothing,' he says. 'As though it never happened.'

'Except you have a scar,' says Linny, with a small smile she immediately straightens.

'Yes,' he says, touching it.

His mother comes around the table to him, as they all watch, and holds his face in her hands. 'Michael,' she says in a voice not quite her own. 'What do you want to know?'

In the morning Michael studies his face again in the bathroom mirror and the scar glitters like ice.

Triptych

1. The Home

Arthur sat with his wife in the cafeteria and stared out the window at the shape of the dead kangaroo lying in the shrubbery. It was mushroom soup today, and his wife added salt, a teaspoon at a time, after each sip. 'When are we going home?' she asked. Outside, the light was fading into the hydrangea bushes, but in here the red-and-white checks of the plastic tablecloths shone fluorescent. Arthur poured water from a carafe into their glasses. 'We are home,' he said.

The kangaroo looked as though it had been attacked by another animal. There didn't seem to be any flattening or crushed bones consistent with a car smash. Just a single slash across its belly, some spilled entrails; the end of its tail was also missing. Perhaps it had been swiped by a car and then, off-balance, had fallen, crawled in through the gates, and been at the mercy of scavengers: dogs, wild cats, maybe even a wedge-tailed eagle. The home was surrounded by bushland, about fifteen kilometres off the main road which itself joined the state highway thirty kilometres away. Peaceful the children called it, a bit isolated, but geez, Art, you don't get quiet like this in the city.

It had been the first thing he'd seen that morning. Awake at five-thirty in a wet bed and on the way to the linen cupboard he'd opened the loungeroom blind and there it was, right under the window. Its soft eyes were open, its sheep-face muddied. The slash along its belly was through two layers of thick skin: a pouch, a female. He'd gone to the front office at nine and informed them; they said Kyle the maintenance man would pick it up on his weekly round. Until then, it would have to stay.

Arthur had shot a kangaroo once, up on Lester's farm at Easter time. Lester, a new farmer then, wasn't all that keen on roo-shooting, but the boys from the neighbouring farms were there and all for it. They'd gone out drunk, riding in the back of someone's ute, clutching borrowed guns and high-beam torches. 'They're a menace,' someone said as if in answer to a secret misgiving. When the time came and the roos were hopping like ghosts through the beams, Arthur had been the only one to get a direct hit. They'd skinned it and cooked cutlets over a fire, throwing the tail and paws to the dogs. Arthur smiled now, thinking about it, and his wife looked at him and laughed, loud and long.

There was craft after lunch – Christmas cards. His wife used a stencil of a Christmas tree and cut a trembly outline. 'Merry Christmas darlings,' she wrote inside and signed *Grandma*. Later he would gather them up and write long messages in them, updates for her children in his neat hand. He would use the address book and write the envelopes, fasten the stamps. And later they would reply with letters or phone calls of their own, and they would feel, he knew, better for the contact.

That night he watched the news and *The Bill*, aware of his wife walking from the door to the bed to the bathroom and back again, telling him at every turn, 'This is where we'll stay for a bit,' or 'A nice room, we'll stay here tonight,' 'Oh look at the bathroom, there's a dear little yellow duck sitting on the sink.' He caught her eye and nodded. Eventually she settled beside him on the couch and told him who was handsome, who a trollop, who a bad man.

They met ten years ago when she moved from the north to be nearer her daughter Marie. He was an elder of the church Marie occasionally visited and was invited over for lunch after the morning service. These kinds of polite invitations weren't uncommon. He was ready for soup and sandwiches, careful Christian chat, maybe a word of advice for some itinerant son. But instead he found Willa, dashing out a blues tune on a piano while the children danced in circles, arm in arm.

'Mum, come meet Arthur, he's an elder,' said Marie. Arthur knew he looked just like an elder, his grey hair shining and swept back, his shirt tucked neatly into belted serge trousers, his glasses, his big flat nodding head. She'd held out her hand. 'Arthur,' she said, 'I'm Willa.' She had a clutch of rings on the hand he shook while nodding to her smiling face.

Three days later and the kangaroo lies still in the shrubbery outside his window, almost a familiar sight now, but slightly changed every day. The body somehow heavier-looking, more bound to the soil in which it rests; burying itself. Tomorrow is the garden-maintenance day and

Kyle will put it in a garbage bag, then into a big skip to be dumped with all the other waste.

His wife looks at him in the new way she has now, from her chair, suspiciously, with an edge of contempt. He has just come from the shower, and wears a white singlet tucked into his trousers.

'Getting fat,' his wife says, looking at his belly. 'You should get a bike, and ride like me and Marcus did.'

It is a name that has been edging into her vocabulary more and more lately, part of the brain's regression through the past the doctors say. Gone is the coyness of those first months, and gone even the steady politeness of their years of marriage. Now she says the name with a hardness in her eye, knowing the trick of jealousy still, and playing it.

When the daughters come to visit, they rifle through old photographs with their mother, an exercise the doctors say is beneficial. Last time, Willa kept a photograph of her ex-husband out from the box and propped it up against a lamp. 'Marcus,' she said with a concentrated familiarity, and touched the eyes of the picture. He put it away again when she wasn't there, and she's forgotten since. Marcus is an angular man, and looked aggressively from the paper at Arthur's softening belly.

He only had five years with her before her mind began to lose its hold on reality. They'd married in a garden and he'd sung for her in his elder's baritone, while the daughters watched indulgently before travelling back to their homes, leaving her in his hands. There was twelve years between them, but no-one had noticed. They lived in a small flat five minutes from the beach. On the first morning of their married life Willa had learned of his habit of rising at dawn to wander the beach and take a dip if the wind was low. She never got used to the alarm clock, even when he bought a small whirring one that tucked under his pillow. 'It is still night,' she would groan. 'The genteel do not rise until nine 'o'clock and take their tea in bed.'

They both became more involved in the church, she taking hold of the children's program, and he leading the choir. Children followed her everywhere like ducklings, cooing at her, pecking at her sleeves. Two or three would often come and spend the weekend, dressing up, eating eggs and cakes, screeching out tunes on the piano and accordion. Arthur would retreat often to his chair, or to the beach, where he would sit and watch the rips from his car, muttering cautions to himself about underwater hazards. He returned home once to find Willa draped in purple staring at an overturned fishbowl and pronouncing each child's future in dour intonations. Afterwards, he'd scolded her mildly, asking her if she thought it very Christian to offer fate in a crystal ball. 'They are impressionable,' he'd said. 'And they believe every word you say, Willa.' She'd laughed, revealing the first inkling of a larger disdain. 'They do not believe anything Arthur. You do not know children, and what they do. It's only when we get older that we must *believe* in something, and disbelieve something else.'

In the chill quiet of the evening, Arthur looks at the kangaroo, for the last time no doubt. Its face has crumpled and ants have taken over those parts where innards have come outwards. It is smaller, and dusty, like an old broken toy. He is half-listening to Willa who has discovered the bedroom again, and is changing the linen for the third time this evening. Usually she will stop at five, exhausted though she doesn't know why, and curl into bed, her mouth gradually slackening and wettening.

'Marie!' she calls suddenly. He realises she is back in their family home, where the daughters grew up, where she and Marcus lived. He opens his mouth to tell her, Marie is not here, we live in a home now, but she continues. 'Marie, your father will be home soon, let's tizzy up the place!' And she giggles in a voice Arthur has never heard. He watches her from the dark alcove as she scampers from the bedroom, disoriented, but finding the stereo in the lounge and his neatly arranged collection of jazz and bebop CDs. She stares at the discs. 'Marie,' she says, faltering. He emerges to take her elbow, and watches the light disappear from her eyes, her shoulders sag. 'Marie's not here,' he says, guiding her. 'It's time for bed, love.'

Lester, Arthur's brother, had come to stay a year into their marriage. Lester's wife had died, he'd left the farm in his sons' care. He'd slept in the spare bedroom, loudly.

Lester's boots thundered around their small house, his shirts were brazen, his voice emerging in shots, like gunfire. Coming home from choir rehearsal one evening, Arthur had found Willa washing his brother's hair in the bathroom basin. Lester, swathed in towel and with foamy head was softening visibly under her touch. And she was laughing, her hair in tangles, their voices echoing tinny around the tiled walls.

It seemed to Arthur he was always opening doors to find Willa another woman, one he did not know. But she was losing control now, and the doors were falling open on their hinges.

In the quiet house, Arthur sits in his chair and flips through the address book beside the phone. Marie has written in her father's phone number, 'In case something should happen to Mum, he would want to know,' and without pausing to think, Arthur dials it.

'Yes?' Marcus answers sharply. Arthur can hear other voices in the background, the tinker of glasses, and laughter.

'Hello? Who is this?'

Arthur shifts to lean forward in his chair and stares at his knees. 'Marcus, good evening, it's Arthur here. Willa's husband.'

'Oh, Arthur,' says Marcus, his voice fading a little. Arthur hears the background noise disappearing as Marcus moves away. 'Is something wrong with Willa?'

'No,' Arthur begins. But stops, staring at his fingers as they lie folded on his knees. 'Well–' he begins again.

'Yes?'

Arthur imagines Marcus's angular face, his eyes impatient, scanning. His impeccable clothes sitting casual on his lean limbs. Not like an elder at all.

'Her Alzheimer's is developing.'

'Yes, yes. Marie keeps me up to date. Has she wandered away or something?'

Arthur closes his mouth tightly and presses his teeth together until his jaw locks and hurts. Why on earth did he call this man?

'Arthur?'

'No, no, nothing like that,' Arthur mutters between his teeth.

There is a pause and he hears Marcus sigh quietly.

'Sometimes,' Arthur begins, 'she does not recognise me.'

'Yes, well, that's to be expected, isn't it?' Marcus answers.

'I mean, she does not expect her husband to look like me. I come into the room and she expects to see...' Arthur falters, presses his fist against his thigh. 'Someone else,' he finishes, defeated.

'Yes?' says Marcus. 'Well, this is what happens. The brain degenerates. She is retreating to the past.'

'I thought,' Arthur stumbles on, bending double on the chair. 'I thought you might like to visit her sometimes. She doesn't have long. I would like to see her...' Arthur scans for the word, as he has seen his wife do. 'Cheerful,' he says.

Marcus is quiet.

'I will have to think about it, Arthur,' he says eventually, sharply. 'And speak to the doctors of course.'

Yes, of course, think about it,' says Arthur, standing up suddenly. 'Well, that's all. Goodnight Marcus.'

'Goodnight.'

Arthur hangs up the phone and takes two paces towards the hallway, then stops and returns.

On an impulse he goes to the laundry and finds a pair of gardening gloves and a trowel, kept although they are useless here in the tended surrounds. He brings garbage bags, goes out the front door and kneels by the kangaroo's side.

Part of the skin on the kangaroo's face has decomposed, showing the tops of its teeth, which are held gritted. Arthur puts on the gloves and touches its fur. The kangaroo's wounds are now black with dirt, its pouch hanging like cloth from where it has been torn. It's tail is a blackened stump. Arthur lays out a garbage bag and, placing his hands beneath the kangaroo's forearms, heaves its dead weight onto the plastic. After it is wrapped, he clears a small plant from the garden and digs with his trowel into the bark-chips and soft soil. He is tired and his knee-bones ache.

He pushes the heavy bundle into its grave and covers it again, replacing the plant carefully so its roots bear it steady.

Kyle will not find the kangaroo tomorrow. It will stay here, under the window, and sink deeper into the earth even once he and Willa are long gone. Arthur goes back inside, replaces the gloves and trowel and sits in his chair, staring out at the darkening garden.

2. The Window

Every afternoon I wait at the tram stop and look up at the lit windows of the hospital.

Lately someone has been looking back.

The first time I saw the figure was two weeks ago, after a late dinner. The wine was in my head; the hospital looked like something from science-fiction, spotlit cranes looming silent, scaffolding crawling up its walls. Most windows were dark, but some glowed their block of white out into the street.

I could only see the person in silhouette, but I knew they were looking at me. On the windowsill I could see a bunch of flowers, and they: shapeless and dark, standing quite still. We continued looking at each other until my tram pulled up and gathered me away.

For a few days I tried to find the window again, but I forgot its exact position. All the windows remained empty.

Then the figure appeared again, this time in the late afternoon. When I saw it, the shape was familiar, a black outline as though from a dream. There was something about the light around the person that made me think of the moon, some quality of whiteness, and they a strange eclipse.

After that I saw the figure every day, when I waited for the tram. It hovered above me, some angel, from its anonymous room.

I'd been into the hospital a couple of times, as a visitor. A friend broke a leg, a bad fracture to the thigh-bone, and we'd walked the halls with our flowers, breathing that sharp wakeful hospital smell. We looked at doors, trying to find the room number, and inadvertently saw the other people behind the other doors, who watched us from their beds, and did not recognise us.

I remember the way the rooms were set up, with two beds against each wall, separated by curtains. The window at the end, with the comfortable chair. The beds, as centrepieces, somehow not as neat as one imagines hospital beds to be. Their sides spilling over, bedside drawers top-heavy with flowers, the awkward imbalance of the drip-machine, the plugs in the walls. Yet everything contained by the smell, which finds its aspect in glints, from the polished floor, from the forced teeth of nurses.

So this is how I imagined this person, who looked out at me from their window. Amongst white hospital debris. Listening to the endless hospital sounds, beeps, hums, crying, sudden shouts, rustles, footsteps. Perhaps they had been there for a long time. Perhaps they had always been there. In the end, there was no telling.

*

She is a woman, I am sure of it. She turned to the side yesterday and I'm certain I saw a faint curve under the shapeless gown, a certain falling of the cloth, a certain grace. I wait for her. If she is not there at the window when I first arrive at the stop, I miss trams until she appears. She arrives like a dream, one moment the window is empty, the next full with her familiar outline. I never see her approach. She is simply there, or not.

I am wondering whether tomorrow I will raise my hand to her, or make some other gesture, to see if she will respond.

Why is she so ill? She does not seem ill. Her movements, slight though they are, are not the slow pained ones of the terminal. Her body, shrouded in its cloak of silhouette-black, which must really be white, does not seem frail. On the contrary, she looks as though she could hold all the weight of the world, and not falter.

*

I have counted how many storeys up her window is, and then how many windows from the side. I think, if I was inside, I could find her.

*

She is not sick in the usual sense. I mean, her body has not been over-run. There is no foreign growth, there is no slow fade, there is no treatment and no cure. She is simply in hospital, amongst the white machines. They keep her there, and they keep her form intact.

Sometimes I think she is a hologram.

Sometimes I think she performs for me.

Yesterday I blinked and when I opened my eyes, the light in her room had gone out. I stared at it. Then I blinked again and the light had returned, with her in the window in a posture of gentle insouciance.

*

I see her every morning and evening now, for at least half an hour each time. I allow myself to be late to work sometimes, if I feel she wants me to stay longer. Once I didn't go to work at all, and stayed outside the hospital all day, snacking from the 7/11 across the street and resting my legs against the tram-stop railing. It was like a picnic. She strolled, or sat, turned the lights on and off, moved her flowers. Spending slow time with her like this is, I feel, good for my soul. I let my breath slow down. I am quiet. There is no need to form words on my lips, no need to battle to be heard. There exists between us in this wordlessness, an understanding that unfolds time and space. She knows this too. Once I tried to show her how I felt. I pointed to myself, then opened my palm and let it float to her in a gesture of dedication, thanks, provision. She remained perfectly still, did not indicate her reception in the slightest way. I understood immediately: there is no *I* to signify here, there is no *you*; there is no space between through which to float flimsy sentiments. We are one, we are one.

*

I have not seen her for three days. Her window remains dark. I continue to wait. I don't know what to do.

*

When she is absent, I am absent. I am no longer present in my body. My boss told me to go home for the day. I went to the hospital and watched the window until my legs gave out from under me. It was the dead of night. My eyes, when I look around, see only squares of dark.

*

I climbed the stairs into the hospital today, found the elevator and travelled six storeys up. I turned left and started counting the doors, but there are rooms I had not expected – a medicine storage room, a nurses' quarters, a bathroom. Do these doors count? I thought I would be able to feel her presence, and be drawn to her, but the hospital smell, contained in glints, outdoes me. I open doors and look into empty, unfamiliar eyes. I bow my head.

Eventually I am stumbling, almost running, upstairs and downstairs, looking into doorways and calling out, not a name since I have none, just a wordless noise. I arrive, panting, at a room with an empty bed by the window, a bunch of flowers on the sill. If I blink I can still see her outline at the window, and if I blink again… does she turn towards me?

I take off my shoes and my jacket. I lie down to rest in the white bed.

*

Every morning I stand at my window and look outside where the traffic and the trams clutter past. I remember being there once, amongst the concrete debris, and the endless outdoor sounds: car horns, tram bells, engines, wind in trees, talk and laughter. It seems a long way down.

3. Grandma – A portrait in fragments

We'd go to meet Grandma at the train station. I'd always wonder
whether I'd be able to recognise her straight away or whether it would
take me a while to adjust to her whitening hair or her smallness. But it
never took me more than a moment to see her purple beret, flowery
calottes, her arms waving madly, "Grandma's here. Over here!"

We'd bring her home in the car and she'd sit with us kids in
the back seat and talk to us more than to Mum and Dad. She would
promise us all the things we knew were Grandma-things: lolly treasure
hunts, tea kisses and the-ay-tre.

A tea kiss was a hot one on the cheek just after a sip of tea. It
left our skin warm and wet and we smelt Grandma's tea-sweet breath.

This was when we were children – those memories you want to hold
on to when things change. Grandma would bring out a bag of lollies
and we'd have to go and wait endlessly in a bedroom until she'd call
out, "Ready!" Then we'd scamper around the house and find jellyba-
bies on the dusty bookshelves and fantales on the window ledges. In
the evening she said she was tired, but Dad would sit at the piano and
we'd sing hymns until dark. We'd go to bed, reluctant but excited,
soothed by Grandma's cracking voice rising and falling from the
loungeroom.

Every other Christmas, we'd drive up the east coast to Culburra where
Grandma lived in a house on stilts, five minutes walk on white sand to
the beach. Everyone would come – four aunties and their three hus-
bands and seven children, and an uncle with his wife and five children. I don't know where they all went at night – we stayed in the
house or slept in a tent on the back lawn. One Christmas Eve my sister
and I were sleeping in a double bed in the spare room, thrilled out of
our wits but at that age before teenager-hood of fake calm. From the
corners of our eyes we both saw Grandma, dressed all in red, come
slowly through the door, feeling at the walls and singing something in
her tuneless low voice. My sister and I stifled shrieks of delighted
laughter. Grandma was fumbling with two packages and dropped one
on the floor before placing them noisily in the pillow-cases we'd laid

out. Still humming discordantly, she left the room and we shoved our heads under the pillows and laughed uncontrollably.

Unable to wait until morning to see what Grandma had brought us, we turned on a lamp and took out the little packages of clumsy crunching cellophane. Each contained nuts and glace cherries, stuck together in a ball, some still with carpet-strands gummed on. We warily picked out a couple of walnuts and pecans to chew on and the episode forever after was known to us as 'the hairy walnut'. We told the story to our school friends in peals of harsh laughter, making Grandma's gesture of spontaneous Christmas magic into something stupid and weird.

Grandma stopped dyeing her hair blonde one year and it became snow-white overnight. She'd touch it carefully and say, 'It turned this lovely soft pure white and it's so much nicer now isn't it?' She'd sit in her new purple outfits or model hats for us and I'd think how vain she was, how girlish. And I would be jealous, like I was of all the other girls who loved clothes and shoes and being pretty with a passion I would never be able to understand.

Recently, when I went to see Grandma, her clothes were stained and she coughed up mucus into a tissue. On the beautiful old mirror next to her bed, the mirror she had catwalked in front of for our admiration, was written: "Today is Monday, 9:04 am. It is a beautiful day and I will see you soon. Love John xxoo." John was Grandma's husband, her new one, not my Grandpa whom I never met. When my father and I saw her it was Wednesday afternoon, but Grandma looked over at the mirror every few seconds and didn't ask us the day or the time.

'And what happens on Mondays?' She said. And we said, 'Well, today you are a bit unwell and you can't go and do the activities.' And she nodded quietly and tucked herself up like a child.

Grandma's the-ay-tre act, the one she did every time there was a family gathering, was 'Lost in the Fog'. She would leave the room with such exaggerated secrecy that we all knew what was coming. Then she'd re-enter with the lights dimmed, a shawl draped over her head and a piece of looped rope trailing from her hand.

'I'm a poor little girl and I'm lost in the fog,
Me and me dog, we're lost in the fog.

Won't some kind gentlemen guide us home?'

She would wander in a circle around the gathering, appealing solemnly to each gentleman, not once releasing her face from its sorrowful gaze, her voice a low wail.

I was confused by the performance as a child, but I saw my father chuckling and my uncles who offered her their arm with a smile, so I smiled too.

A few years ago, when Grandma's Alzheimer's was still in its early stages and hadn't yet been named, we were having lunch with her and John and one of my aunties, Lil. Lil was talking about how much she and her daughter loved reading the Harry Potter books. I was saying that I hadn't read them, but I'd seen one of the movies. Grandma said, 'What are we talking about?' and Lil said 'Harry Potter books.' Grandma said, 'Oh yes, I've got a few books by him. Yes I like him a lot, he's a very clever man.'

Her bluff was transparent, even to herself when she saw the awkward way we looked at each other. I thought about all the times I had used the same tone, the same bluff, about my knowledge of music or movies or sport and I warned myself to be more careful.

Everyone said, when I was fourteen and starting to thicken in various places, that I had Grandma's body. A too-long lean upper half and squat legs with ugly ankles and curvy toes. Grandma's toes fascinated me as a child. They sat splayed, with huge gaps between the second and third, the fourth and fifth, the others jammed together, curled like tadpoles against each other. I looked at my own toes beginning to curve and separate, and dreaded the day when I would have Grandma's toes.

I suppose when you are young and living in a sort of trance of isolated study, you begin to forget that the art of dialogue once sprang from talk itself. On our recent visit, the one where it was always 9:04 am, Grandma sat in her rucked bedclothes and questioned each of us over and over. I found new ways of saying 'I'm studying for a PhD at Melbourne University,' and new ways of responding to, 'Oh, you're the clever one aren't you, and that's a very good school, isn't it?'

John came in to say good morning, although he was sick himself. Grandma questioned him immediately.

'And what is this place? Is this where I live now?'

'Yes, Del, this is your room. This is where you stay.'

'And I can't get out of bed because I have what they call Alzheimer's disease.'

'No, normally you can get out of bed and do things, Del, but today you have a bad cold and you need to rest.'

Grandma smiled wryly. 'Who invented Alzheimer's disease anyway?'

My father grinned back, 'I suppose it was Mr Alzheimer himself.'

'I wish he hadn't,' said Grandma.

And I could hardly believe that conversations like this occurred.

That night I heard on the news about a breakthrough discovery for the treatment of Alzheimer's. It said that one in four people over the age of sixty die of the disease. It didn't seem to me a thing that one could die from, a loss of memory. The report explained the degeneration of the brain and how the treatment would prevent, or slow, this erosion. In another report, later in the week, green vegetables and exercise were attributed to a later and slower onset of the disease.

Whenever I read fiction or see a film involving a person with dementia I find myself terribly shaken up. In fact I need to interrupt myself to note that *terribly*, such a Grandma word, with the "r's" rolled together into a shapeless "ww" sound, an impediment that made her sound more intelligent and refined, rather than less. But the books, like Ian McEwan's *Saturday* when Henry Perowne visits his mother and captures the strange mad poetry of their chat, and that film *Iris* with Judi Dench playing a slowly deteriorating Iris Murdoch... Perhaps not such a great book, not a great film, but they left me reeling in their wake, sobbing for the pity of it. For my Grandma.

My grandfather I did not know, except for dark photographs from which he smiled sternly, but cheekily with the chin and dimples I recognise in my father and aunts, in myself. His father started him off studying economics and then teaching in a primary school. They wrote letters to each other full of cricket scores and sudden adolescent bursts of 'Alas father! I hate the study of money! I want to be a poet, I want to study the arts!' He eventually became a minister and wrote sermons in which he quoted Shakespeare. He met my grandmother when he was editing a small newspaper. She inadvertently wore red, black and white to the interview, the colours of my grandfather's beloved St Kilda Saints. He hired her.

This is one story I've heard, and there are precious few. He died when my father was only twenty-one, leaving him an engraved watch. He missed my sister's birth by a year. I often wonder what it would have been like to have known this man, a man of letters, a man of God, his severe black pictures, his stern smile with that Roald Dahl twinkle in the middle of his eyes.

It's 9:04 and my father takes a book down from Grandma's shelf, which is laden with photos, dolls and teddy bears. It is a book of songs and poems that my Auntie Lil has made. These are the songs Grandma remembers, once you begin the opening line. My father begins 'There is a green hill far away,' and instantly Grandma's face alights and she sings along, word-perfect, in her wavering monotone. It is a scene I watch, not knowing the words. My father and his mother singing a hymn in this small room, in this retirement home, the nurses brash, their eye makeup too thick, the food in packages, my grandmother with a pile of dirty tissues. When the song ends, she begins again, her eyes no longer jumping mystified from one strange visitor to another, but resting on my father as he sings with her, and will sing again and again until it is time for lunch.

A grand lady, her unusual children living in faraway cities, her grandchildren pondering and enormous, with their brush-stroked memories, their few memories. This man my father, who came from her, who *is* her.

I saw my father once pulled over by policemen, for no particular reason. It was at night, us three in the back, and they shone a torch into the car like on TV. The light was pointing down onto his hands, which we all saw shaking like an old woman's. There was no problem – they looked at his license. He answered their questions quickly in a breaking voice. When the policeman heard my father speak, something about his manner changed. It was a strange equation the policeman was trying to make – this car, its squeal, its patchwork of colours, this man, his red nose, his unkempt beard tousled over a flannel shirt – with *this* voice: high, clipped, biting down on a well-read vocabulary. When my father's stomach rumbled, like a school of whales on the ocean floor, the policeman looked up into the sky, as though the puzzle might be solved in the arrangement of the stars. We were silent, going home, having seen something we knew shouldn't be mentioned – the emergence of a stranger from he who we thought familiar.

Why had he never learnt the art of chatting platitudes, I sometimes wondered. Why had he not adopted that jovial tone of a man with another man, even if a policeman? I imagined the household of his upbringing to be one of lessons and truths, hard-won, but enacted delightfully; a mixture of *Little Women*, *The Goon Show*, *Biggles* comics and the Bible. What my grandmother retains, far more than the gentle repetition of social niceties, are songs, poems and jokes. My father, too, has a head full of quotations and stories, was thus dumbfounded by the everyday authority of the police.

Grandma will say to you again and again, 'And what is it all for then?' You will tell her, 'We're all gathered here to see you. We're your family.'

'My family?' she will say. 'But I don't know any of these people.'

She will put her face down in her arms on the table in the middle of the restaurant.

She will say she is tired and has such a headache.

When you rub her back and talk over her head about a wheelchair, a pill, she will tell you to shut the hell up.

You did not know Grandma knew these words.

Boxes begin arriving one day when John decides to move from his self-care unit into the nursing home facility with Grandma. There is no room anymore for the shelves of books. Grandma's Will begins to take effect before she has passed away. I receive an enormous 1890 dictionary, which I look through carefully, marvelling at its tracing-paper delicacy, along with a 1902 copy of Don Quixote, some Whitman poems, and Conrad's 'Tales of Hearsay'. All these, I place between bookends next to the blue china windmill from great-Oma Clement, and the miniature tea set from Oma. A shelf of relics then, objects from the dead. Except Grandma, she isn't dead yet. She is simply far away, and she does not know who I am.

It's 9:04 again and you will crouch beside her and she will lift her head from her arms.

'It's ok, Grandma, we are all a lot bigger now. You probably remember me from when I was only a little girl.'

'Which one are you?'

'I'm Elizabeth, Lizzie. I'm Jeff's daughter.'

And for a moment her eyes will not flicker away.

'Haven't you become a lovely young woman. Such an elegant dress.'

And you will spin around, in front of the lying mirror, and touch your hair, and Grandma will smile, and she will see herself continue.

*

Conclusions

Elizabeth has a virtual white page in front of her. It is even furnished with a lifelike paper-shadow that runs along its right edge and across its base. At her fingertips, the alphabet, in an arrangement someone researched once, she assumes, and figured out to be the most convenient for typing. Maybe it was the other way around; maybe the letters fell like that, and the convenience is something we've learned. In any case, the possibility of writing and the possibility of not writing co-exist here with the tools and the means, the convenience, right in front of her. She compares the situation to the thought experiment known as Schrödinger's Cat. A hypothetical cat is placed inside a hypothetical steel chamber for one hour along with a vial of poison. Also in the chamber is a very small amount of a radioactive substance. If a single atom of this substance decays, a relay mechanism will trip a hammer which will, in turn, break the vial of poison and kill the cat. Until the observer lifts the cover from the box, both possibilities, alive cat and dead cat, exist together in a 'mixture' of states. At the point at which the lid is lifted from the box and the cat is examined, a quantum wave of probability collapses. It can never be known what the outcome would have been if it were not observed – thus Schrödinger posited that observation itself affects an outcome. Come to think of it, the philosophical riddle "If a tree falls in a forest" poses a similar conundrum of the effect of the observer, and probably more eloquently. But Elizabeth prefers the claustrophobia of the steel chamber and the poison when she thinks about the quantum possibilities of the blank page.

She imagines a writer locked in a room, sound-proof and windowless. In front of her, blank pages and a pen. We leave her there for a day. Until we open the door, we cannot know if she has put pen to page, or if the paper remains blank. What is the hammer that triggers her to write? Is she a vessel, a vial, of odourless acid, even the vapour of which will stop the breath of cats, and of any other creature, let alone the potency of its liquid form as it seeps into the quill? And what if she does not write – what work does poison do to the inner walls of such a vessel? Is the possibility of writing a random occurrence, as with the decaying of the radioactive substance? Elizabeth imagines the door opening at the end of the day, and the observer entering the room. She imagines the observer and the writer locking eyes for a moment before their attention is turned to the pages on the desk, blank or otherwise.

Foreground and Background

This book was initiated and informed by one image, that of a hand holding a pen, hovering above a blank page. Reading Coetzee' novels, the hand became that of the Magistrate who, after staring at the page trance-like for three days, cannot find what it is he is meant to write. The hand became the cleft mouth of Michael K, who feels heavily the burden of the absence of his story, its performance, and its rewards. The hand was Susan Barton's who continues to tell and tell, though she does not know why or to whom; and Friday's, who derides his empty maw by donning the vestments of author, and holding a dripping quill. The hand became dying Mrs Curren's who writes because she feels betrayed, and the master's, Fyodor Dostoevsky's, who writes in order to betray. It became David Lurie's and hovered above an unfinished libretto, before the pen was dropped and replaced by the quivering fur of a dying dog. Then the hand belonged to Elizabeth Costello, an ageing and celebrated author, who after travelling the world delivering lectures, finds herself locked in a claustrophobic room with her subject, her character, and her observer, Paul Rayment. Throughout the book they produce together, the pen changes hands, is wrested from hands, is left forgotten on the table, and is taken up again like a dropped stitch. The two circle each other. They hinge, in the end, on an unlikely word: love. "Almost at random she has lighted on him," thinks Rayment, "as a bee might alight on a flower or a wasp on a worm; and somehow, in ways so obscure, so labyrinthine that the mind baulks at exploring them, the need to be loved and the storytelling, that is to say the mess of papers on the table, are connected" (Coetzee 2005: 238).

Underneath all of these other hands and mouths is the hand and mouth of Coetzee. Throughout this book I have tried to present the argument that the trigger which causes Coetzee to choose 'to-write' over 'to not-write' is the possibilities and repercussions of that very choice. He returns over and again to the moment of writing, to questions of the value of writing, or speaking, to the relationship between writing and observing, or reading, and to what happens after someone writes. Although these ideas have informed all of his work, the recent Elizabeth Costello novels address issues of writing and reading explicitly, thus making them targets for criticisms like Mars-Jones's 'Is it actually a novel?'

In many ways the ideas presented in this book have not been concluded at all, but are still actively echoing throughout literary and academic circles. Where I began in 2004 having read and seen the remarkable links between only *Disgrace* and *Elizabeth Costello*, Coetzee has since published a short story and a novel which reprise the character of Costello – 'As a Woman Grows Older' and 2005's *Slow Man,* a new collection of essays, *Inner Workings*, in 2007, the 2007 novel *Diary of a Bad Year,* and a third fictional autobiography *Summertime* in 2009. *Diary of a Bad Year*, which this book has not been able to fully address, centres around an eminent seventy-two-year-old Australian writer and his neighbour Anya whom he employs as secretary. In a striking, almost experimental move, Coetzee split the novel into three strands which appear on the page all at once, separated typographically by lines and fonts. The first is a collection of the writer's political essays; the second, his personal musings about Anya; and the third, Anya's own reflections on the ensuing events. Reading the book, then, becomes a matter of flicking backwards and forwards, holding one's thumb a few pages behind, or ahead, choosing the order and direction in which one wants to hear the story. As commented in *The Age*, "The whole nature of the experience will come under scrutiny – you will be forced to consider the nature of the relationship between yourself as a reader, the book as an object, its content, and the writer" (Steger 2007: 29).

It's clear, then, that Coetzee is still deeply interested in the processes of reading and writing as subjects for novels and that any study of his work at this time will necessarily be an ongoing process.

However, within the context this book set for itself, which was to examine the Costello novels acting as Postscript to Coetzee's previous body of work, both fiction and non-fiction, some conclusions have been reached regarding the nature of that moment of putting pen to paper. One conclusion reached, as demonstrated in 'The Author Divided', is that the moment of writing signals the moment of divi-

sion. While the pen is still hovering above the page, before the trip
hammer shatters the vial, the page and the author might still be considered distinct, whole entities. They might also be considered passive
entities. When the pen is brought to the paper, the white page becomes
a backdrop for the pen-marks; it is divided. This image serves as a
template for other kinds of divides within the author. The action, or
activity, of the pen on the page strikes a divide between 'writing' – the
active foreground – and 'being written' – the passive background. If
we transpose the verbs to include the author, we could perhaps phrase
the divide as being between the one-who-writes and the-writing-one;
or between the action of writing and being 'a writer'. *Elizabeth
Costello* and *Slow Man* make the distinction overtly by establishing
Costello as 'a writer' from the outset and confirming the label through
mention of her books and her fame. However the question posed in
the parable-language of *Costello*'s Lesson 8 – what is a writer without
her books? – has been asked in a number of Coetzee's previous books,
even those which didn't centre around the figure of a famous writer.
The character of Michael K, for instance, is one of those who, after a
day in the locked room, would give back to the observer a pile of
blank pages, a lidded pen. This does not mean he does not think about
storytelling:

> Always, when he tried to explain himself to himself, there re-
> mained a gap, a hole, a darkness before which his understanding
> baulked, into which it was useless to pour words. The words were
> eaten up, the gap remained. His was always a story with a hole in
> it: a wrong story, always wrong. (Coetzee 1983: 150-1)

And later:

> It struck him too that his story was paltry, not worth the telling,
> full of the same old gaps that he would never learn how to bridge.
> Or else he simply did not know how to tell a story, how to keep
> interest alive. (Coetzee 1983: 240)

And again:

> They want me to open my heart and tell them the story of a life
> lived in cages. They want to hear about all the cages I have lived
> in, as if I were a budgie or a white mouse or a monkey. And if I
> had learned storytelling at Huis Norenius instead of potato-
> peeling and sums, if they had made me practise the story of my

> life every day, standing over me with a cane till I could perform
> without stumbling, I might have known how to please them. I
> would have told the story of a life passed in prisons where I stood
> day after day, year after year with my forehead pressed to the
> wire, gazing into the distance, dreaming of experiences I would
> never have, and where the guards called me names and kicked my
> backside and sent me off to scrub the floor. When my story was
> finished, people would have shaken their heads and been sorry
> and angry and plied me with food and drink; women would have
> taken me into their beds and mothered me in the dark. Whereas
> the truth is that I have been a gardener, first for the Council, later
> for myself, and gardeners spend their time with their noses to the
> ground. (Coetzee 1983: 247)

Where perhaps Michael feels he has failed his observers by not providing them with a story, he is essentially exploring the strange divide
between writing and being a writer. The moment of writing is excruciating both for one who considers himself, his background identity, a
gardener, and for one who can consider herself to be, after being
called so, a writer. Both anticipate, as the pen hovers, the paradox of
their foreground and their background – what they are doing and who
they are. The conclusion this book reaches is that this moment of division occurs within the author as they put pen to page, and that this division is explored acutely and repeatedly throughout Coetzee's works.
Through its analysis of Coetzee's books, this study therefore reaches
conclusions about both Coetzee's abiding preoccupations, as established plainly in the Costello books, and about the nature of writing
itself. Often the two intertwine, as with the relationship described here
between the self and writing.

The key text upon which the idea of the moment of divide
hinges is Coetzee's one-and-a-half page essay 'A Note on Writing,'
which introduces the idea of the three-way voice: active, middle, passive, as pertaining to the verb 'to write'. "To write (active) is to carry
out the action without reference to the self…To write (middle) is to
carry out the action (or better, to do-writing) with reference to the
self" (Coetzee 1984b: 11). This idea, with its linguistic premise, is
carried to every level of the divided author that this book nominates:
the author is both particular person and common passageway; the author is both enacting a performance of literature, and catching
glimpses of the Law of literature; and the author is both human and
divine. In each case, the divide could be restated in terms of active
tense – particular, performance, human – and passive tense – com-

mon, Law, divine. And in each case, the author must take her place in the middle voice, making references to herself – her action, her inaction.

In an extract from his 2007 novel *Diary of a Bad Year* published in the *New York Review of Books*, Coetzee's attention to the broader repercussions of the linguistic nuance of tense can be seen once again. It appears both in the details, the content of our author-character's manuscript on the origin of the state, and in the outer context of his meeting with the 'celestial' Anya, who he employs as secretary. As with *Elizabeth Costello*, the reader is in flux between reading and absorbing a text, and being introduced to the life of its author. The eye and mind may never rest upon a written idea – often a grand and polemical idea: "Democracy does not allow for politics outside the democratic system. In this sense democracy is totalitarian" (Coetzee 2007c) – without it being concurrently aware of the idea's particular human origin. Thus the middle self-referencing voice within the divide of active and passive appears once again. Also as in *Elizabeth Costello*, the divide is heard within the texts themselves, as with that between metaphor and analogy, or literature and philosophy, in the Animal Lessons. In *Diary of a Bad Year*, our author, after quoting La Boétie on voluntary servitude, writes the following:

> In an important respect La Boétie gets it wrong. The alternatives are not placid servitude on the one hand and revolt against servitude on the other. There is a third way, chosen by thousands and millions of people every day. It is the way of quietism, of willed obscurity, of inner emigration. (Coetzee 2007c).

The three-way voice, then, also finds its way into our author-character's political ideas: once again content is echoed by and intertwines with form.

Late Style
Something peculiar to reviews of *Elizabeth Costello* and particularly *Slow Man*, was how many reviewers felt compelled to motion towards the books these novels should have been or wanted to be. Often reviewers spoke of the novels as though they were shadows of their fully realised selves, had been somehow thwarted along the way. Most reviews also, however, praised the books and their author generously

and indicated the impression they had that the books, according to their internal logic, *couldn't* be written in any other way. Without mentioning it explicitly, it is clear that reviewers were trying to do two contradictory things at the same time: to see the books as distinct new entries onto the literary scene, and to see them as the latest work by Nobel-prize-winner J. M. Coetzee. The two were often difficult to negotiate.

Having made reference to Said's article 'Thoughts on Late Style,' in the conclusion to the section 'Divided and Divined,' and mentioning throughout the book the influence of Coetzee's position and 'name' upon any impressions and interpretations of his work, the idea of late style features in another of this book's conclusions. From the outset I chose to view *Elizabeth Costello* and *Slow Man* as jarring 'Postscripts' to Coetzee's previous body of work – books which prompted a re-reading, a re-appraisal of Coetzee's recurring themes and preoccupations. The particular ways in which these books were decidedly different from the others raised inevitable questions about the effects that great success, upheaval, a new country, and ageing were having on Coetzee's reasons for choosing 'to-write' over 'to-not-write'.

With the publication of *Diary of a Bad Year*, another novel which challenges and pushes against categorisation, Coetzee seemed to seal his received persona as a difficult, confusing, problematic and, most of all, *untimely* writer. Adam Mars-Jones who was quick to criticise *Elizabeth Costello*, "It's very novel, but is it actually a novel?" is quick again in his similar criticism of *Bad Year* (Mars-Jones 2007: 304), calling it "a series of fragmentary essays tweaked into a fictional framework. Its ambitions to three-dimensional status are fitful – it bears the same relationship to a novel as a hologram does to a sculpture". The most telling of his comments, however, comes at the end of his review where he writes, "There are many suitable responses to the award of a Nobel, dignified silence among them. But posing as a failure isn't a good idea. You should get that out of your system before the call from Stockholm". There are interesting assumptions lying behind these statements: firstly that winning the Nobel prize necessarily puts an author in a position of 'response,' secondly that there is a correct response, and thirdly that Coetzee's response is incorrect – 'unsuitable' and 'undignified'. On the other end of the scale is the far more favourable appraisal of Elizabeth Lowry in *The Times*, whose article sees *Bad Year* positioned seamlessly amongst his other fiction and criticism: "In its skilful deployment of characters who have a rich significance beyond their individual function, its wry exploration of the failures of reciprocity between the self and the other, and its examination of philosophies of community, atonement and sacrifice, this generic cross-breed stands up well next to Coetzee's previous books" (Lowry 2007). Two perspectives, then, which are equally arguable: that Coetzee's latest books represent a break with, a turning abruptly from, a formerly distinguished and illustrious career, or that the books are the evolution of, the organic metafictive versions of, those previous, more naturalistic works.

This book's conclusions on questions like these are indebted to Edward Said's book *On Late Style: Music and Literature Against the Grain*, published posthumously (late, in fact) in 2006. As far as I am aware there has been neither an expression for, nor a significant study of the event or concept of 'late style' beyond this book and its subjects. Said himself is indebted to the late works of Theodor Adorno, who coined the term 'late style' in his essay 'Late Style in Beethoven,' and who continued the theme in his book *Philosophy of New Music*. Said's book, at least its first few chapters, could in fact be read as a commentary or explication of Adorno's writings, aware as it is that "No one needs to be reminded that Adorno is exceptionally difficult to read... he is slow, unjournalistic, unpackagable, unskimmable" (Said 2006: 14-15). Adorno and Said also write about the aforementioned contradiction reviewers tackle between newness and lateness: "What [Adorno] looked for in style was the evidence he found in late Beethoven of sustained tension, unaccommodated stubbornness, lateness and newness next to each other by virtue of an 'inexorable clamp that holds together what no less powerfully strives to break apart'" (15).[9] Again, tension is sustained by virtue of inexorability, a sense that the work could not have been produced in any other way; in other words, when reading Coetzee's latest books one feels the weight of his other books resting behind them – as though it is an old book, dressed up with a new cover and made topical, as though it is an anachronism.

---

[9] Said is quoting Theodor Adorno's 'Late Style in Beethoven' (tr. S. Gillespie) in Richard Lepper (ed.) 2002. *Essays on Music*. Berkeley, Los Angeles and London: University of California Press: 186.

Diary of a Bad Year, which once again pre-empts critical objections by internalising them, includes exchanges such as the following between the secretary Anya and 'JC' an ageing author:

> Why do you write this stuff? Why don't you write another novel instead? Isn't that what you're good at, novels?
> A novel? No. I don't have the endurance any more. To write a novel you have to be like Atlas, holding up the world on your shoulders and supporting it there for months and years while its affairs work themselves out. It is too much for me as I am today. (Coetzee 2007a: 47)

And later, mulling over an idea for a short story, JC writes, "Of late, sketching stories seems to have become a substitute for writing them...Is one of the consequences of growing old that one longer needs the thing itself, that the idea of the thing suffices?" (149) Both of these excerpts make a connection between an ageing subject and the fragmentation of objective form. As one grows older, approaches death, is the indication, the artform as 'world,' as a fully realised, and most importantly *independent* 'thing itself,' becomes unsustainable. Rather, what is brought to life are the rudimentary musings, those shadowy thoughts that exist inseparable from the mind of the would-be Creator. These ideas on the imposition of the subject and fragmentary form of late style are also elucidated by Adorno, as seen by Said:

> Impending death is there, of course, and cannot be denied. But Adorno's stress is on the formal law of Beethoven's final compositional mode...This law reveals itself to be a peculiar amalgam of subjectivity and convention... Adorno says:
>
> Death is imposed only on created beings, not on works of art, and thus it has appeared in art only in a refracted mode, as allegory... The power of subjectivity in the late works of art is the irascible gesture with which it takes leave of the works themselves. It breaks their bonds, not in order to express itself, but in order, expressionless, to cast off the appearance of art. Of the works themselves it leaves only fragments behind, and communicates itself, like a cipher, only through the blank spaces from which it has disengaged itself. Touched by death, the hand of the master sets free the masses of material he used to form; its tears and fissures, witnesses to the finite powerlessness of the I confronted with Being, are its final work. (Said 2006 10-11, quoting Adorno 1993: 105)

In trying to articulate how, and perhaps why, Coetzee's latest novels are markedly different from his previous body of work, this book aligns itself with Said's and Adorno's rhetoric of late style. The impression they give as gestures towards fully realised worlds is one which indicates, at every point, an allegory of death, of foreshortening, of re-coursing towards subjectivity. Said summarizes Adorno on Beethoven's late works:

> They do not fit any scheme, and they cannot be reconciled or resolved, since their irresolution and unsynthesized fragmentariness are constitutive, neither ornamental nor symbolic of something else. [They] are in fact about 'lost totality,' and are therefore catastrophic…For Adorno, *lateness* is the idea of surviving beyond what is acceptable and normal; in addition lateness includes the idea that one cannot really go beyond lateness at all, cannot transcend or lift oneself out of lateness, but can only deepen the lateness. (Said 2006: 12-13)

If, for reviewers like Mars-Jones, then, Coetzee's latest works are unacceptable, unsuitable, undignified, in their hybridity, their fragmentation, then they reflect integral elements of Adorno's 'late style,' which itself reflects the breaking apart of the façade of Creator, in favour of the tears and fissures of the subjective.

The Wrong Question

Something which seems appropriate to appear at the end of a book is a conclusion about questions. Throughout Coetzee's books, both recent and other, characters are faced with and ask themselves many questions, often of a complicated ethical nature. In *Disgrace*, David Lurie asks, 'Do generations of racist governments, tyranny, genocide, poverty and indignity justify, even necessitate, my daughter's silence after her rape?' In *Master of Petersburg*, Fyodor asks, 'Even though by writing, I will commit abominations and betrayals of those I have loved, yet must I not still write, in order to save myself?' Elizabeth Costello asks, 'Should horrible things remain locked behind closed doors, or is there some good that can come of their spread, through acts of writing and reading, across the landscape of human imagination?'

When readers are faced with questions like these, an instinctive response is to remove them from the circumstances from which they arose and to try to think about them in an objective, philosophical way. Another response is to presume that it is Coetzee, behind a series of tricky diversions like character and plot, who is actually asking the question, and to then criticise Coetzee for asking questions like these in the first place. Another conclusion this book has reached concerns the nature of embodiment, and the repercussions embodiment has for the traditional separation of fiction, or 'creative' writing, and theory, or philosophical writing. Both of the above responses to complex ethical questions treat their original context as negligible, treat the characters who ask them as convenient mouthpieces, ploys, treat the surrounding story as a structure, an analogy, within which the question may be asked. Whittling away, in this manner, a story's details – its face, its objects, its texture and touch – in order to ask a question which may be considered real, or universal, is contrary to everything novels like these want to do. As I argued in the section on 'The Ethics of Embodiment,' Elizabeth Costello does not see figures of speech like analogy and metaphor, the novelist's tools, to be the means towards clarifying universal truths, towards reasonable answers. Rather, they are in themselves sites of truth, moments of clarity. In the same way, making up a story, inventing a character, giving her things to say, questions to ask – these activities in themselves argue for the reality of imagination and the importance of bodied ideas.

All these arguments have been posed, and probably won, before, by proponents of post-structuralist theories of validity, such as Paul Dews's description of Derrida's view of literary interpretation: "not as a matter of penetrating to an ultimate, objectifiable truth, but rather of being caught up in an endless 'happening of meaning' which transcends the distinction between subject and object" (Dews 1987: 12). What we have in Elizabeth Costello is a character who asks the wrong question – the unanswerable, indeed unreasonable ethical questions, 'Why should my life be valued more highly than an animal's?' 'Should an old man hanged be left alone or should his story be retold?' – while being simultaneously aware that they are wrong, and that their purpose is not to be answered but to signal herself as asker. She embodies her wrong questions – her indecision, her scrawling messy pages, her quavering, her hypocrisy, all attest to it. This kind of practising theory, a character aware of her position as both perceived mouthpiece for ideas and as living contradiction – an embodied post-structuralist even – challenges the boundaries between creative and critical writing at multiple points. It is a melancholy, desperate, way to write, pre-empting critiques, undercutting the fictional world, blocking, at every point, an easy path to read. But at this point, as Coetzee's last three novels indicate, the drive and sincerity of this kind of practised-theory seems inevitable, and persistent. It's my hope, and the conclusion of this book, that writing like this continues, and that readers will not pluck the wrong questions from it, that they will dispense with the term 'hybrid' to use of these sorts of novels, as though purebred theory has crossed with purebred fiction and produced a mutt.

Postscript: *A Bad Year*

Lately Elizabeth has been crying for no reason.

She sat down to read, in a regular place, at a regular time, on the couch after dinner. She read a poem by Dorothy Porter called 'Egypt'. Even before she had finished the first four-word line the tears were dripping down the backs of her eyes, her mouth was trembling at its corners, her cheeks gorged with blood. Her partner stopped what he was doing to attend to her, to sit closer, to ask. 'I'm sick of being sad all the time,' she said. 'I want my feelings to have their logical stimulants in the outside world, but it is as though they are completely random, uncontrollable.' Later she speaks to her mother, who was long ago diagnosed with bipolar disorder and has been taking antidepressants for over twenty years. 'Is it the Pill?' Elizabeth asks. Her mother can put things so nicely in a calm voice. 'Darling, sometimes you may be on the brink of being depressed. Different things can push you over that brink. The chemical stimulant of the Pill might be one of those factors.' They talk quietly about her concerns and the things which are causing her stress at the moment. Elizabeth does not want to talk about herself this way, in the way her parents talk about each other, with words like 'routine' and 'change' and 'lifestyle'. Isn't she stronger than that? Is she suddenly a patient?

The feeling, when she is in the midst of it, is close to panic. Her breath comes in long gasps in between racking sobs. The sadness is overwhelming, but worse is the fear. In the face of it, Elizabeth finds herself without control, and without a single word she could use to tell it. This is the most terrifying part: the way it takes away all her expression, and leaves her wholly silent, empty, helpless. Sometimes all she needs is the warm arms of her partner, whose words, "It's ok, sweetie, everything's ok," are less important than the smiling calm voice he uses to say them. Sometimes, while holding her, he will tell her of ordinary things, "I've been thinking I'll get a haircut soon," "I won that LP on eBay," "Walking to work today, I bumped into a man. We both knew we would bump into each other, for metres in advance, but neither of us paused." These little stories, which she listens to intently, the tears drying on her face, calm her breathing, and lull her. The dark dread which sat in the pit of her stomach slowly melts. And always, afterwards, she thinks about *having been helped*. The passive tense mirrors her own feeling of passivity.

There is another talisman which helps her. It is a letter from her father, who also suffers. He gives his advice apologetically, knowing the ways it could be construed as patronizing or self-serving. The part she reads, nodding at it in between breaths that come in shudders, goes: "In my experience, you can't fight depression, so I have found the best thing to do is to give in to it. This is also a kind of victory – it takes the depression off-guard, because it is wanting and expecting you to fight. It thrives on the power it has over you, the inequality. I guess it is a kind of fight, but fighting by pure passivity." What is it that has bred in her the idea that it is shameful to be passive, to be weak, to submit? More than all the forms of media she could list that hail triumph, strength, and an active fight as praiseworthy qualities of a person, particularly of a woman, the feeling of shame comes from her parents. But not in the way one might think. Her parents were never those who shouted from the sidelines, who rewarded their children with money or ice-cream for every 'A' on their report-card, who pushed them into classes and activities in order to see them, eventually, succeed. Success did not, in fact, hold importance for them at all. Her father had once been a botanist, he held a PhD and taught at the university, he wrote chapters in books. Her mother had been an occupational therapist, she'd worked with the intellectually disabled. But Elizabeth remembers these past lives only vaguely. Now, and for years now, her parents have lived in a state of passivity, letting life sweep over them in waves, submitting to pain. It was this that Elizabeth, as every child does, rebelled against.

But now she finds herself using the advice, clinging to it even, as the inexplicable panic surges across her vision. *Just give in*, she tells herself. *Let it ride its course. This too shall pass!* And with these phrases, her throat unclenches, her breathing eases. The slow seeping pain of sadness remains, but the fear subsides, and she endures.

She reads another poem, this one by Gregory Day, which has the line: "Fact is no-one quite knows what's going on but it's like God said to Job: '*The discipline man needs the most is to learn his submission to unreason.*'" Again, submission is the task she sets herself. She collects these words, she has become a *help-collector*. She is no longer ashamed for her weakness, as she realises this is the only thing that helps: to be limp in the face of adversity, to let it come, to submit, to watch it pass. In that, there is a kind of victory. She imagines herself a piece of kelp, stuck limpet-like into the ocean floor, and swaying with the swells, collapsing, and recovering.

Lady Chandos too, she turns towards in order to find the safety of common ground. *Always it is not what I say but something else!* The agonised imperfection of the sentence comforts her; those nebulous nouns – *it, something else* – echo her own hands as they cast about for words, her mind as it jitters in panic in the face of something nameless. The history of the words also comforts her, their transition across time and pen. It strengthens the notion she has that the feeling comes from somewhere beyond her own psychology, that it emerges, like exploding stars, like the first bubbling cells, from somewhere primordial.

The unreasonable crying lasts for a few days before she returns to a relatively upright position, back in the world of words, from which she can view the encounter. Elizabeth is surprised at herself for writing about this most personal of experiences for an audience of strangers. While she writes (her fingers darting without question to their black clicking keys) she mocks herself. *Kelp*, she snickers, *have you even seen kelp face-to-face? Have you touched it?* She answers primly: I recall a slippery leatheriness, like the seatbelt in a car. *Like the seatbelt in a car*, her inner Chandos groans. *And what's this: like exploding stars, like the first bubbling cells. What a conceit. Not just a conceit, a lie.* But everything is a lie, she counters. If there is a truth somewhere, then it is characterised primarily by its inexpressibility. It is not what I say. Always, it is something else. *And you're using this borrowed tool of self-awareness to negate all your metaphors? Why can't you just write? Why can't you be a real writer – relaxed with metaphor, at home with comparative description? Just let things be!* But I want to be honest. *You just said everything is a lie.* I want to be honest about all the lies. *This is becoming tedious. No reader is inter-ested in this inner debate.* Coetzee did it, just read *Slow Man. Coetzee has won the Nobel Prize, have you?*

And so it goes on.

If there is one thing she could take from all this writing, from more than three years of reading and writing, it's this: lurking at the back of every bound text, under its cover, behind its spine, between its lines, in the spaces of the letters, there is a long loud argument, there is pain, there is doubt, there is a relentless to-ing and fro-ing. And like hot mud springs – *like hot mud* – a smooth surface may erupt into tumult at any time, it may break apart. Books look like answers – they sit on the shelf colourful and neat. But at every point a writer will be asking a series of unanswerable questions: why write? what good does it do? what is its value? These questions split apart the regular going-along of a story, just as the same questions interrupt the regular intake of breath, the regular lifetime of waking and sleeping.

*

References

Adorno, Theodor. W. 1993. 'Late Style in Beethoven' (tr. S. Gillespie) in *Raritan: A Quarterly Review* 13(1): 102–107.

—. 1967. *Prisms* (tr. Samuel and Shierry Weber). London: Neville Spearman.

Agamben, Georgio. 1993. *Stanzas: word and phantasm in Western culture* (tr. R. L. Martinez). Minneapolis: University of Minnesota Press.

Attridge, Derek. 2004. *J. M. Coetzee and the Ethics of Reading: Literature in the Event*. Chicago and London: University of Chicago Press.

Apuleius. 1998 *The Golden Ass* (tr. EJ. Kenney). London: Penguin.

Baldacchino, Lewis. 1991. *A Study in Kant's Metaphysics of Aesthetic Experience: Reason and Feeling*. New York: The Edwin Mellen Press.

Barry, Peter. 1995. *Beginning Theory: An Introduction to Literary and Cultural Theory*. Manchester and New York: Manchester University Press.

Barth, John. 1982. *Sabbatical*. London: Secker and Warburg.

Barthes, Roland. 1977. *Image, Music, Text* (tr. S. Heath). London: Fontana Press.

—. 1974. *S/Z* (tr. R Miller). New York: Hill & Wang.

—. 1972a. *Critical Essays* (tr. R. Howard). Evanston: Northwestern University Press.

—. 1972b. *Mythologies* (tr. A. Lavers). London: Jonathan Cape.

Battersby, Christine. 1989. *Gender and Genius: Towards a Feminist Aesthetics*. London: The Women's Press.

Beardsworth, Richard. 1996. *Derrida and the Political*. London: Routledge.

Blanchot, Maurice. 1999. *The Station Hill Blanchot Reader: Fiction and Literary Essays* (tr. L. Davis, P. Auster and R. Lamberton) Ed. George Quasha. Barrytown: Station Hill.

—. 1998. *Death Sentence* (tr. L. Davis). Barrytown: Station Hill.

Blanchot, Maurice. 1995 *The Work of Fire* (tr. C. Mandell). Stanford: Stanford University Press.

—. 1986. *The Writing of the Disaster* (tr. Ann Smock). Lincoln and London: University of Nebraska Press.

—. 1971. *Friendship* (tr. E. Rottenberg). Stanford: Stanford University Press.

Borges, Jorge L. 1970. *The Aleph and Other Stories* (tr. NT. di Giovanni). New York: E. P. Dutton & Co.

Brophy, Kevin. 2007. 'Writing PhDs: Integrational Linguistics and a New Poetics for the PhD' in *TEXT: Journal of Writing and Writing Courses* 11(1). Online at http://www.textjournal.com.au/april07/brophy.htm (consulted 29.09.2012).

Calinescu, Matei. 1993. *Rereading*. New Haven and London: Yale University Press.

Calvino, Italo. 1988. *Six Memos for the Next Millenium*. New York: Vintage.

—. 1981. *If on a Winter's Night a Traveller*. London: Picador.

—. 1968. *Cosmicomics* (tr. W. Weaver). London: Abacus.

Carey, Peter. 1997. *Jack Maggs*. St Lucia: University of Queensland Press.

Clarke, Stella. 2003. 'An invitation to think' in *The Weekend Australian* (6 September 2003): B29.

Clendinnen, Inga. 1999. *Reading the Holocaust*. Cambridge: Cambridge University Press.

Coetzee, J. M. 2007a. *Diary of a Bad Year*. Melbourne: Text Publishing.

—. 2007b. *Inner Workings: Literary Essays 2000-2005*. Sydney: Knopf.

—. 2007c. Extract from *Diary of a Bad Year* in *The New York Review of Books* (July 19 2007). Online at: http://www.nybooks.com./articles/archives/2007/jul/19/diary-of-a-bad-year/ (consulted 28.09.2012).

—. 2007d. 'Exposing the beast: factory farming must be called to the slaughterhouse' in *The Sydney Morning Herald* (22 February 2007): 17.

—. 2005. *Slow Man*. Sydney: Knopf.

—. 2004. 'As a Woman Grows Older' in *The New York Review of Books* (January 15 2004). Online at http://www.nybooks.com/articles/archives/2004/jan/15/as-a-woman-grows-older/ (consulted 28.09.2012)

Coetzee, J.M. 2003a. *Elizabeth Costello*. Sydney: Knopf.

—. 2003b. 'Fictional Beings' in *Philosophy, Psychiatry & Psychology* 10(2): 134.

—. 2003c. 2003 Nobel Lecture. Transcribed from video at http://nobelprize.org/literature/laureates/2003/coetzee-lecture.html

—. 2002. *Youth*. London: Secker & Warburg.

—. 2001. *Stranger Shores: Essays 1986–1999*. London: Secker & Warburg.

—. 1999a. *Disgrace*. London: Vintage.

—. 1999b. *The Lives of Animals*. Princeton: Princeton University Press.

—. 1997. *Boyhood*. London: Secker & Warburg.

—. 1996. *Giving Offense: Essays on Censorship*. Chicago: The University of Chicago Press.

—. 1995. 'Meat Country' in *Granta: Food – the Vital Stuff* (52). Ed. Ian Jack. London: Granta Publications.

—. 1994. *The Master of Petersburg*. London: Secker and Warburg.

—. 1992. *Doubling the Point: Essays and Interviews*. Ed. David Attwell. Cambridge and London: Harvard University Press.

—. 1990. *Age of Iron*. New York: Random House.

—. 1989. 'Idleness in South Africa' in Armstrong, N. and Tennenhouse, L. (eds.) *The Violence of Representation: Literature and the History of Violence*. London and New York: Routledge.

—. 1988a. *White Writing: On the Culture of Letters in South Africa*. New Haven and London: Yale University Press.

—. 1988b. 'The Novel Today' in *Upstream* 6(1): 2-5.

—. 1986a. *Foe*. Harmondsworth: Penguin.

—. 1986b. 'Into the Dark Chamber: The Novelist and South Africa' in *The New York Times Book Review* (January 12 1986). Section 7: 13.

—. 1984a. 'Truth in Autobiography' *Inaugural Lecture* (New Series 94). University of Cape Town.

Coetzee, J. M. 1984b. 'A Note on Writing' in Daymond, M.J, J.U. Jacobs and M. Lenta (eds.) *Momentum: On Recent South African Writing*. Pietermaritzburg: University of Natal Press: 11-13.

—. 1983. *Life and Times of Michael K*. London: Secker & Warburg.

—. 1981. 'Time, Tense, and Aspect in Kafka's "The Burrow"' in *Modern Language Notes* 96(3): 556-579.

—. 1980. *Waiting for the Barbarians*. Harmondsworth: Penguin.

—. 1977. *In the Heart of the Country*. London: Vintage.

—. 1974. *Dusklands*. London: Vintage.

Craven, Peter. 2005. 'Salman the Ghost' in *The Age* (October 15 2005): 5.

Dante Alighieri. 1998. *Inferno* (tr. E. Zappulla). New York: Pantheon Books.

Debelle, Penelope. 2004. 'Coetzee's curt answers' in *The Age* (March 3 2004). Online at http://www.theage.com.au/articles/2004/03/02/1078191320576.html (consulted 29.09.2012).

Deleuze, Gilles. and Parnet, Claire. 2002. *Dialogues II* (tr. H. Tomlinson, B. Habberjam and ER. Albert). New York: Colombia University Press.

de Man, Paul. 1986. *The Resistance to Theory*. Minneapolis: University of Minnesota Press.

Derrida, Jacques. 1992. 'Before the Law' in Attridge, Derek (ed.) *Acts of Literature*. New York and London: Routledge: 181-221.

—. 1978. *Edmund Husserl's Origin of Geometry: An Introduction*. NewYork: Stony Brook.

Dews, Peter. 1987. *Logics of Disintegration: Post-structuralist Thought and the Claims of Critical Theory*. London: Verso.

Dovey, Teresa. 1988. *The Novels of J. M. Coetzee: Lacanian Allegories*. Craighall: A. D. Donker.

Duncan, Robert. 1993. *Selected Poems*. New York: New Directions Books.

Durrell, Lawrence. 1960. *Clea* London: Faber and Faber.

Fauchery, Antoine (images), Dianne Reilly and Jennifer Carew (text). 1983. *Sun Pictures of Victoria: The Fauchery-Daintree Collection*. South Yarra: Currey O'Neil Ross/Library Council Victoria.

Falconer, Delia. 2005, 'The Great Unspooler,' *The Monthly* (November): 57–8.

Fineman, Joel. 1981. 'The Structure of Allegorical Desire' in Greenblatt, Stephen J (ed.) *Allegory and Representation: Selected Papers from the English Institute*. Baltimore: John Hopkins University Press. 26-61.

Flaubert, Gustave. 1992. *Madame Bovary* (tr. G. Wall). London: Penguin.

Gardam, Jane. 1986. 'Books: the only story,' in *The Sunday Times* (September 7 1986).

Gaut, Berys. 2004. 'The Ethical Criticism of Art' in John, E. and McIver Lopes, D. (eds.) *Philosophy of Literature: Contemporary and Classic Readings – An Anthology*. Malden, Oxford and Carlton: Blackwell. 355-362.

Hadfield, Andrew, Dominic Rainsford and Tim Woods (eds.). 1999, *The Ethics in Literature*. London and New York: MacMillan/St. Martins.

Head, Dominic. 1997. *J. M. Coetzee*. Cambridge: Cambridge University Press.

Hofmannsthal, Hugo. Von. 1986. *The Lord Chandos Letter* (tr. R. Stockman). Vermont: The Marlboro Press.

Holland, Norman N. 1993. 'Reader-Response Criticism' in Preminger, A and Brogan, TVF (eds.) *The New Princeton Encyclopedia of Poetry and Poetics*. Princeton: Princeton University Press: 1383.

—. 1975. *The Dynamics of Literary Response*. New York: The Norton Library.

Holub, Robert. C. 1992. *Crossing Borders: Reception theory, Poststructuralism, Deconstruction*. Wisconsin: The University of Wisconsin Press.

—. 1984. *Reception Theory: A Critical Introduction*. London: Methuen.

Houellebecq, Michel. 1999. *Atomised*. London: William Heinemann.

Huggan, Graham and Stephen Watson (eds.). 1996. *Critical Perspectives on J. M. Coetzee*. London and New York: MacMillan.

Hugo, Richard. 1979. *The Triggering Town: Lectures and Essays on Poetry and Writing*. New York: W. W. Norton.

Jakobson, Roman. 1987. *Language in Literature*. Eds. Pomorska, K. and Rudy, S. Cambridge & London: Harvard University Press.

John, Eileen and Dominic McIver Lopes (eds.). 2004. *Philosophy of Literature: Contemporary and Classic Readings – An Anthology*. Malden, Oxford and Carlton: Blackwell.

Kafka, Franz. 1958. *Wedding Preparations in the Country and Other Stories* (tr. E. Kaiser, E. Wilkins, W. Muir, E. Muir). Harmondsworth: Penguin.

—. 1994. *The Trial* (tr. I. Parry). London: Penguin.

Kant, Immanuel. 1960. *Observations on the Feeling of the Beautiful and Sublime* (tr. JT. Goldthwait). Berkeley and Los Angeles: University of California.

—. 1914. *Kant's Critique of Judgment* (tr. J. H. Bernard). London: Macmillan. Online at <http://oll.libertyfund.org/?option=com_staticxt&staticfile=show.php%3Ftit le=1217&chapter=97555&layout=html&Itemid=27> (consulted October 5 2012).

Lacan, Jacques. 2002. *Écrits: A Selection* (tr. B. Fink, H. Fink and R. Grigg). New York: W. W. Norton.

—. 1977. *Écrits: A Selection* (tr. A. Sheridan). London: Tavistock/Routledge.

Lang, Berel (ed.). 1988. *Writing and the Holocaust*. New York: Holmes & Meier.

Lee Hermione. 2003. 'The rest is silence' in *The Guardian* (August 30 2003). Online at http://books.guardian.co.uk/reviews/generalfiction/0,6121,1031735,00.html (consulted 30.09.2012).

Levi, Primo. 1984. *The Periodic Table*. New York: Schocken Books.

Lewis, Peter. 1980. 'Types of tyranny' in *The Times Literary Supplement* (November 7 1980): 1270–71.

Llosa, Mario V. 2001. *The Feast of the Goat*. London: Faber & Faber.

Lodge, David. 2003. 'Disturbing the Peace' in *The New York Review of Books* (November 20 2003) 50(18). Online at http://www.nybooks.com.ezp.lib.unimelb.edu.au/articles/archives/2003/nov/20/disturbing-the-peace/ (consulted 19.10.2012).

Lorenzo, Olga. 2002. 'Dissection of a Despot' in *The Age* (June 15 2002). Online at http://www.theage.com.au/articles/2002/07/15/1026185150564.html (consulted 30.09.2012).

Lowry, Elizabeth. 2007. 'Coetzee's ruffled mirrors' in *The Times Literary Supplement* (August 22). Online at http://www.the-tls.co.uk/tls/reviews/fiction/article746325.ece (consulted 19.10.12).

Lyotard, Jean-François. 1988. *The Differend: Phrases in Dispute* (tr. G. Van Den Abbeele). Minneapolis: University of Minnesota Press.

Macaskill, Brian. 1994. 'Charting J. M. Coetzee's Middle Voice' in *Contemporary Literature* 35(3): 441–75.

Macherey, Pierre. 1978. *A Theory of Literary Production* (tr. G. Wall). London: Routledge.

Malcolm, Janet. 1993. *The Silent Woman: Sylvia Plath and Ted Hughes*. London: Picador.

Marais, Michael. 2006. 'J. M. Coetzee's *Disgrace* and the Task of the Imagination' in *The Journal of Modern Literature* 29(2): 75-93.

—. 2000, ' "Little Enough, Less than Little: Nothing": Ethics, Engagement, and Change in the Fiction of J. M. Coetzee' in *Modern Fiction Studies* 46(1): 159–182.

Markovits, Benjamin. 2005. 'Out on a limb' in *New Statesman* 51 (September 12 2005): 2.

Mars-Jones, Adam. 2007. 'Even Nobel winners can make mistakes' in *The Observer* (August 26 2007): 304.

—. 2003. 'It's very novel, but is it actually a novel?' in *The Observer* (September 14 2003). Online at http://observer.guardian.co.uk/review/story/0,6903,1041470,00.html (consulted 30.09.2012).

McCullers, Carson. 1943. *The Heart Is A Lonely Hunter*. Harmondsworth: Penguin.

McLaughlin, Robert. L. 2004. 'Post-postmodern discontent: contemporary fiction and the social world' in *symploke* 12(1-2): 53-69.

Miano, Sarah. E. 2005. '*Slow Man* by J. M. Coetzee' in *The Times* (September 3 2005). Online at http://cma.staging-thetimes.co.uk/tto/arts/books/article2454045.ece (consulted 30.09.2012).

Midgley, Mary. 1981. *Heart and Mind*. London: Routledge.

Miller, Andrew. 2005. 'Breaking the Rules' in *The Financial Times Weekend Magazine* (September 3 2005): 32.

Milosz, C. 1988. *New and Collected Poems: 1931-2001*. New York: HarperCollins.

Mitchell, Susan. 2000. *Erotikon*. New York: HarperCollins.

Muller, John and William Richardson. 1982. *Lacan And Language: A Reader's Guide to* Écrits. New York: International Universities Press.

Murnane, Gerald. 1987. *Landscape with Landscape*. Ringwood: Penguin.

Nagel, Thomas. 1974. 'What is it like to be a bat?' in *The Philosophical Review* 83(4): 435-50.

Neumann, Anne W. 1990, 'Escaping the "Time of History"? Present Tense and the Occasion of Narration in J. M. Coetzee's *Waiting for the Barbarians*' in *The Journal of Narrative Technique* 20(1): 65–86.

Osborne, Ben. 2004. 'Feet on the ground, head out of the clouds' in *Lumen: The University of Adelaide Magazine* (Winter 2004): 9.

Parker, David. 1990. *The Mighty World of Eye: Stories/Anti-Stories*. Brookvale: Simon and Schuster.

Pinchevski, Amit. 2001. 'Freedom from Speech (Or the Silent Demand)' in *Diacritics* 31(2): 71–84.

Poulet, Georges. 1969. 'Phenomenology of Reading' in *New Literary History* 1(1): 53–68.

Rätt, Djurens. 2004. 'Animals, humans, cruelty and literature' in *Satya Magazine* (May 2004).

Reiss, Timothy. 1992. *The Meaning of Literature*. Ithaca and London: Cornell University Press

Riemer, Andrew. 2003. 'Elizabeth Costello' in *The Sydney Morning Herald* (September 13 2003) Online at http://www.smh.com.au/articles/2003/09/12/1063341766203.html?from=storyrh s (consulted 30.9.2012).

Robbins, Jill. 1991. 'An Inscribed Responsibility: Levinas's *Difficult Freedom*': review of *Difficult Freedom: Essays on Judaism* by Emmanuel Levinas. *Modern Language Notes* 106(5): 1052-1062.

Ryle, Martin and Kate Soper. 2002. *To Relish the Sublime? Culture and Self-realisation in Postmodern Times.* London and New York: Verso.

Said, Edward. 2006. *On Late Style: Music and literature against the grain.* New York: Pantheon.

—. 2004. 'Thoughts on Late Style' in *The London Review of Books* (August 5 2004) 26(15): 3–7.

Sartre, Jean-Paul and Benny Lévy. 1996. *Hope Now: The 1980 Interviews* (tr. A. van den Hoven). Chicago: University of Chicago Press.

Schelling, Friedrich W. J. 1980. *The unconditional in human knowledge: four early essays* (tr. F. Marti). Lewisburg: Bucknell University Press.

Schlink, Bernard. 1997. *The Reader* (tr. CB. Janeway). New York: Pantheon Books.

Schott, Webster. 1982. 'At the Farthest Outpost of Civilization' in *The Washington Post: Book World* (May 2). 12(18): 1–3.

Schuessler, Jennifer. 2003. 'The novelist and the animals: J. M. Coetzee's unsettling literature of animal rights' in *The Boston Globe* (October 12 2003). Online at http://www.boston.com/news/globe/ideas/articles/2003/10/12/the_novelist_ and_the_animals/ (consulted 30.09.2012).

Schwarz, Daniel R. 1999. *Imagining the Holocaust.* New York: St. Martin's Press

Singer, Peter and Renata Singer (eds.). 2005. *The Moral of the Story: An Anthology of Ethics through Literature.* Malden, Oxford and Carlton: Blackwell.

Singer, Peter. 2004. Interview with Andrew Denton on *Enough Rope* ABCTV. Aired 4/10/2004 Transcript online at http://www.abc.net.au/tv/enoughrope/transcripts/s1213309.htm

—. 1999. 'Reply' to Coetzee's *The Lives of Animals*. Princeton: Princeton University Press: 85-91.

—. 1975. *Animal Liberation: A New Ethics for Our Treatment of Animals.* London: Jonathan Cape.

Steger, Jason. 2007. 'Pay attention' in *The Age* (June 9 2007): A29.

Stocks, A. G. 1991. 'Charles Simic' in Chevalier, Tracy (ed.) *Contemporary Poets – 5th edition.* Chicago: St. James Press.

Svevo, Italo. 1993. *As a Man Grows Older* (tr. B. de Zoete). Los Angeles: Sun and Moon Press.

Taylor, David J. 2005. 'Codes for the enigma of survival' in *The Independent* (September 2 2005).

Taylor, Jane. 1999. 'The Impossibility of Ethical Action' in *Mail & Guardian* (July 23-9 1999): 25.

Tompkins, Jane. 1989. 'Me and my shadow' in Leitch, Vincent (ed.) *The Norton Anthology of Theory and Criticism.* New York and London: W. W. Norton: 2129-2143.

Tresize, Thomas. 2001. 'Unspeakable' in *The Yale Journal of Criticism* 14(1): 39–66.

Webb, Jen. 2009. 'Inbetween Writing: Philosophy and catachresis' in *TEXT Archive* (April 2009). Available online: http://www.textjournal.com.au/archive/webb1.htm (consulted 19.11.2012).

West, Paul. 2004. 'The Novelist and the Hangman: when horror invades protocol' in *Harper's Magazine* (July 2004) 309(1850): 89–94.

—. 1989. *The Very Rich Hours of Count von Stauffenberg*. New York: The Overlook Press.

Wood, James. 2003. 'A Frog's Life' in *London Review of Books* (October 23 2003) 25(20). Online at http://www.lrb.co.uk/v25/n20/james-wood/a-frogs-life (consulted 30.09.2012).

Worthington, Kim L. 1996. *Self as Narrative: Subjectivity and Community in Contemporary Fiction*. Oxford: Clarendon Press.

Yardley, J. 2003. '*Elizabeth Costello* Review' in *The Washington Post* (16 Nov 2003).

Žižek, Slavoj. 1989. *The Sublime Object of Ideology*. London and New York: Verso.

Index